THE MORAL VISION
OF
DOROTHY DAY

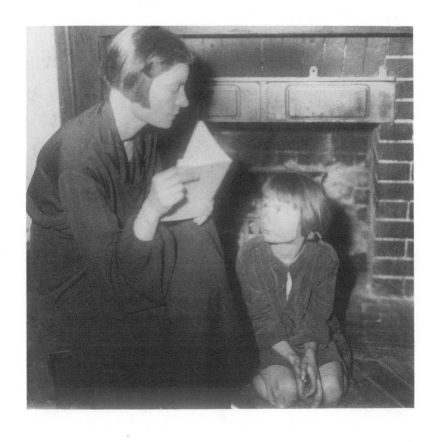

Dorothy Day and Tamar, ca. 1932. Courtesy of the Marquette University Archives.

THE MORAL VISION
OF
DOROTHY DAY

A Feminist Perspective

June O'Connor

CROSSROAD · NEW YORK

1991

The Crossroad Publishing Company
370 Lexington Avenue, New York, NY 10017

Printed in the United States of America

Library of Congress Cataloging-in-Publication Data

O'Connor, June.
 The moral vision of Dorothy Day : a feminist perspective / June
O'Connor.
   p. cm.
 Includes bibliographical references and index.
 ISBN 0-8245-1080-1
 1. Day, Dorothy, 1897–1980. 2. Converts, Catholic—United States—
Biography. 3. Church and social problems—Catholic Church.
4. Catholic Church—Doctrines. 5. Feminism—Religious aspects—
Christianity. 6. Catholic Worker Movement. I. Title.
BX4705.D283026 1991
267'.182'092—dc20
 [B]   90-15583
                                                     CIP

For Harry Hood
and
Meagan O'Connor Hood

CONTENTS

ACKNOWLEDGMENTS

MANY PERSONS HAVE AIDED ME in the work of this book and I am grateful for the community of interest and support they have provided. The University of California, Riverside, Academic Senate Committee on Research supported the work with research funds. Phillip Runkel and colleagues, staff at the Marquette University Dorothy Day-Catholic Worker Collection, welcomed me to the archive and made my research stay pleasant and productive. Students at the University of California, Riverside, have aided my work as research assistants and interested inquirers; I am especially grateful to David Burroughs, Cynthia Carr, Debi Covert-Bowlds, Medeita Gregg, Leslie Hayes-Bolter, and Linda Curran Thomas.

In conversations and correspondence that had varying purposes, colleagues have voiced questions or offered observations that stimulated my thinking and moved me to reexamine a question or clarify a conviction. In these ways, sometimes knowingly, sometimes unknowingly, they have assisted me as I lived with the questions that shape this study. For this I thank Daniel Berrigan, S.J., Margaret Farley, Christine Gudorf, Mark Juergensmeyer, Sallie McFague, Douglas Parrott, Constance Parvey, Brian K. Smith, Katherine Tillmann, and John Howard Yoder. The Gender and Methodology Research Group, initially supported by the American Academy of Religion, has become a resource of increasing importance, and I am grateful for the critical reading of sections of this book by Sheila Briggs, Emily Culpepper, Karen King, Maura O'Neill, Ann Taves, Karen Torjesen, Anne Wire, and Barbara Brown Zikmund. Karen O'Connor, a professional writer and my sister, provided a steady, important, interested presence throughout the project. Joy Cronk, Isabel Gutierrez, and Kim Sharp typed portions of the manuscript with expert attention and patiently instructed me in the ways of the computer. Justus George Lawler, editor, encouraged the project from an early stage and contributed important suggestions that improved the manuscript.

Conversations with Catholic Workers aided my understanding of and feeling for the work and lifestyle launched by Dorothy Day. I am grateful to Workers and guests at the Catholic Worker Hospitality Kitchen and Ammon Hennacy House of Hospitality in Los Angeles, Immanuel House of Hospitality of Santa Ana, California, Casa Maria House of Hospitality in Milwaukee, Wisconsin, and with Workers from a wide variety of Catholic Worker Houses of Hospitality who convened at the International Meeting of Catholic Workers in Nevada, November, 1987. Workers from the United States, Europe, and Canada gathered in Las Vegas to celebrate the ninetieth anniversary of Dorothy Day's birth and to register a non-violent protest at the Nevada Nuclear Test Site.

Some of the materials in chapters one, two, and three have appeared elsewhere. An earlier version of chapter one can be found in *Religion* under the title, "Dorothy Day as Autobiographer." An abbreviated version of chapter two was published in *Horizons, Journal of the College Theology Society*, as "Dorothy Day and Gender Identity: The Rhetoric and the Reality." Chapter three contains some material common to "Dorothy Day's Christian Conversion," *Journal of Religious Ethics*.

The work of writers who are also mothers is supported, protected, and enhanced by a network of people who probably do not realize the important role they play in the making of a book. By inviting my daughter, Meagan, to participate in their lives and play in their homes, many families provided unexpected research and writing time for which I have always been grateful. For this I thank Desireé and Paul Benoit, Annette Compton, Mary and the late (and greatly missed) Richard Dooley, Penny and Dennis Guler, Loretta and Bob Holstein, Rita and Kevin O'Connor, Eva and Philip O'Connor.

To Harry and Meagan, husband and daughter, friends, playmates, and occasional critics, to whom this book is dedicated, I give abundant thanks—for respecting my work time and for distracting me from it at just the right moments, for asking questions about the project and even reading portions of it, and especially for the loving and the laughing that give zest to our working and living together.

INTRODUCTION

It is no longer possible to study religious practice or religious symbols without taking gender—that is, the cultural experience of being male or female—into account. And we are just beginning to understand how complex the relationship between religion and gender is.

> Caroline Walker Bynum,
> *Gender and Religion*, 1–2[1]

The uniqueness of feminist theology lies not in its use of the criterion of experience but rather in its use of *women's* experience, which has been almost entirely shut out of theological reflection in the past.

> Rosemary Radford Ruether,
> *Sexism and God-Talk*, 13

We have learned that sensitivity to the concrete experience of women . . . is the foundation for feminist ethics.

> Barbara Hilkert Andolsen,
> Christine E. Gudorf,
> Mary D. Pellauer, eds.,
> *Women's Consciousness,*
> *Women's Conscience*, xiii

The construction of theory in religious ethics must continually be fed by the lives of women as well as the

---

1. In the text and notes, I have abbreviated references. Full bibliographical information is contained in the Bibliography.

1

lives of men if it is to be adequate, accurate, illuminating, and useful (the necessary criteria for any compelling theory). Conversely, theoretical frameworks are
necessary lenses enabling us to see those lives more
vividly and in relation to one another.

June O'Connor

The central question raised by women's history is:
what would history be like if it were seen through the
eyes of women and ordered by the values they define?

Gerda Lerner,
The Majority Finds Its Past, 162

T HESE QUOTATIONS SUGGEST MY INTERESTS in studying Dorothy
Day. As a university student, professor, and scholar throughout my
adult life, I have been drawn to and driven by questions of religion and
ethics. In recent years, these interests have been related to and informed by questions raised from the developing fields of feminism and
women's studies. It is quite natural, I suppose, that I would find Dorothy Day of interest, a person impelled by religious and ethical concerns
who felt she had something distinctive to say about social issues precisely because of her experiences and perspectives as woman and
mother.

Becoming familiar with the life stories of persons like Day has been
extremely important in my own search for clarity and value. Such
stories stretch me to sort out the questions that bother me and to face
new and important questions I have not asked myself; they also serve
as vivid models for selecting and internalizing values, negotiating conflicts, making decisions, and living life in relation. I have been particularly intrigued by persons whose religious convictions take
sociopolitical expression. Although the context for my life has consistently been education, it was a pastor, resister, and civil rights leader,
Martin Luther King, Jr., who stimulated my interests in ethical reflection and analysis. His writings on the ethics of social change led me to
study Indian activists and writers Mahatma Gandhi and Sri Aurobindo
Ghose, as I sought to identify the ways in which religiously impelled
social activists put their moral worlds together. Themes of social conflict, nonviolent resistance, and a variety of peacemaking efforts led me
to an interest in the liberation theologies of Latin America, and these, in

turn, led me to examine the literature of women's liberation.[2] I felt a native appreciation for the ideals of the women's movement as I came to know it in the 1970s.

It is this cluster of interests—in religion, ethics, social activism, nonviolent resistance, peacemaking, and women's issues—that led me to look closely at Dorothy Day (1897–1980) whose life and writings were permeated by religio-ethical-social concerns, norms, and ideals. I ask of Day's work a number of questions raised by the newly developing field of feminist religious ethics.[3] As a woman who lived through two feminist movements in the twentieth century—the suffragist campaign prior to 1920 and the women's movements of the sixties and seventies—Dorothy Day's view of these movements and responses to them invite attention. Given her widely recognized concern for justice (for laborers, for migrant workers, for young men subject to conscription), I wonder how these public commitments relate to the quests for equality, participation, partnership, and justice that have marked the women's movements.

I also wonder about ways in which this woman, driven by moral and religious concerns for more than six decades, might speak to contemporary debates regarding women and moral discourse, and women and moral theory, as reflected in current discussion about the "ethic of justice" and the "ethic of care." I ask if her moral discourse has a distinctive tone, if her moral voice a distinctive message. I want to focus on her thoughts about moral attitude, desire, conviction, and argument. I am curious about her understanding of power and how she herself exercised power and authority. I wonder what characterizes her underlying moral vision and how she put that together. I also wonder how reflective she was about these questions, how self-critically conscious.

That gender is a formative force that shapes perceptions and participation in culture, religion, and society, and in the construction and dissemination of knowledge, is widely documented, as the bibliography in this book illustrates. In addition to gender, attention is given also to

---

2. See O'Connor entries in the Bibliography. Given my movement from King to Gandhi and Ghose to feminist literature, I was interested to read that Gandhi, while in England in 1906, said that he learned the power of noncooperation from the suffragists. See Dale Spender, *Women of Ideas*, 531. Devaki Jain's article "Gandhian Contributions Toward a Feminist Ethic" further illustrates the mutual interests between Gandhian work and feminist work.

3. For a variety of voices and issues being addressed in feminist religious ethics, see Barbara Hilkert Andolsen et al., eds., *Women's Consciousness, Women's Conscience: A Reader in Feminist Ethics*. For the work of one particular feminist religious ethicist who addresses a variety of related issues, see Beverly Harrison, *Making the Connections: Essays in Feminist Social Ethics*.

ways in which class, race, ethnic heritage, religion, and region are important factors for understanding. Noting these particularities of experience enables our generalizations and universal human claims to have greater credibility. If theories about human life, behavior, viewpoint, and value are to be accurate and adequate, they must incorporate these particularities which are at one and the same time limiting and illuminating lenses for looking at life. Attention to issues of class, race, gender, ethnic and religious heritage is to be directed to the subjects, events, assumptions, and arguments studied, to be sure, but also to the ways these particularities inform the perspective and affect the thought patterns, assumptions, questions, and orientations of the scholars examining their materials.

Reflecting on these particularities with respect to my own standpoint and approach as I study Dorothy Day—as well as the standpoint and approach which I discover in Day—leads me to acknowledge that my own work is necessarily affected by my white, middle-class, Irish-American, Roman Catholic Christian roots, planted firmly in the United States during the second half of the twentieth century. My work is shaped, however, not only by these inherited circumstances and processes of socialization but also by my chosen commitments to continue and to relativize these particularities through disciplined learning, self-critical analysis, and a commitment to understanding persons of other social locations, intellectual orientations, and religious inheritances.

To speak of Dorothy Day and feminism or to examine Dorothy Day in feminist perspective requires explanation, for the words *feminist* and *feminism* continue to alienate and discomfort many people, even some who share feminist identities and interests.[4] "Feminist" and "feminism" regularly evoke images of political protest, confrontation and accusation, heavy critique calling for radical change. The image is one in which feminists flare, nonfeminists flinch—not exactly the setting for dispassionate inquiry and dialogue. Is not "feminist research," the critic charges, an example of oxymoron, a phrase that conjoins contradictories?

Mary Pellauer's description of feminism is particularly helpful for those of us who engage in feminist research.[5] It provides a generalized but accurate description of what we do at the same time that it moves us beyond entrapment in political imagery and highly charged emotion. In

---

4. Ann Patrick Ware acknowledges this, for example, in "Change and Confrontation within the Roman Catholic Church," 36.

5. Surveys of feminist research in religion over the past thirty years include the following: Anne E. Patrick, "Women and Religion: A Survey of Significant Literature, 1965–1974"; Anne Barstow Driver, "Review Essay: Religion"; Carol Christ, "The New

brief, feminist research is a mode of inquiry and reflection driven by a curiosity about women. Pellauer writes,

> Feminism is not, in my view, a set of *a priori* answers, nor a commitment to a particular ideology. It is rather a willingness to follow questions wherever they lead us. Feminism insists upon a commitment to listening with open ears to women's experience. . . . It is thus more a method for creative inquiry than a set of predetermined points. Feminism *is* a commitment to women's well-being, . . . but the substance of women's well-being is not necessarily known in advance.[6]

Indeed, the substance of women's well-being constitutes one item for debate among feminists themselves who come to their feminism from diverse geographical, ethnic, cultural, philosophical, and religious roots. Since contemporary feminism in the United States and Europe has its philosophical and political roots in the Enlightenment, which held "liberty, equality, and fraternity" as revolutionary goals based on the belief that "all men are created equal," much of feminism's impulse has been to extend these values to include women. Women and men of color as well as white women, also wage laborers and the very poor, have had to insist on access to these values, and in doing so have spawned a variety of revolutions in the nineteenth- and twentieth-century United States: the abolition of slavery, women's suffrage, the civil rights/black pride/black power movements, the feminist movement, the American Indian movement and the farm workers' campaigns, together with various advocacy actions to expand opportunities for the poor, illiterate, and homeless. Feminists thus bring to their work not only a curiosity about women as women but also a critical eye with respect to how society and culture have been defined and shaped, and by whom.[7]

Feminist Theology: A Review of the Literature"; Gayle Graham Yates, "Spirituality and the American Feminist Experience"; Barbara Hilkert Andolsen, "Gender and Sex Roles in Recent Religious Ethics Literature"; June O'Connor, "Rereading, Reconceiving, and Reconstructing Traditions: Feminist Research in Religion." *Inheriting Our Mothers' Gardens: Feminist Theology in Third World Perspective*, ed. Letty Russell et al., concludes with an annotated bibliography on African, African-American, Asian, Asian-American, Hispanic, and Third World materials.

6. "Moral Callousness and Moral Sensitivity," in Barbara Hilkert Andolsen et al., eds., *Women's Consciousness, Women's Conscience*, 34. For discussions of the impact of feminist inquiry on other disciplines, see Berenice Carroll, ed., *Liberating Women's History*; Elizabeth Langland and Walter Gove, eds., *A Feminist Perspective in the Academy*; and Dale Spender, ed., *Men's Studies Modified*.

7. Angela Davis, *Women, Race and Class*; Zillah R. Eisenstein, *Capitalist Patriarchy* and *Feminism and Sexual Equality*; Marilyn Massey, *Feminine Soul*.

Resources for feminism are not limited to those of the European and American Enlightenment but include traditions that predate the Enlightenment watershed. Feminists interested in the role religion has played in the lives of women often find mixed messages in the traditions studied. Claims affirming women's value, dignity, and equality with men in the spiritual order are not uncommon. Claims about women's disvalue and subordination, as well as social practices regulating and restricting women's participation, are also not uncommon.[8] Untangling these threads in a given time or place to determine what is distinctive to a given community and what is generalizable continues to be one of many important tasks being addressed in women's studies in religion.[9] Some feminist inquiries focus on historical discovery and recovery. Others attend to reinterpreting the past on the basis of these discoveries and interpreting the present in light of rethinking the past. Still other feminist studies are comprised largely of claims and supporting arguments directed to effect significant change in our understandings, assumptions, beliefs, and practices.[10]

One of many items on the agenda of feminist religious ethicists is attention to women as moral agents, moral analysts, and moral critics. As a relatively recent perspective, feminist religious ethics brings a

---

8. Rosemary Ruether demonstrates these two motifs in the Christian theological tradition, identified as "equivalence" and "subordination," in a concise and excellent article on "Christianity" in *Women in World Religions*. The theme of equivalence refers to that point of view that acknowledges that men and women are different in various respects yet equal in value; the theme of subordination refers to the point of view and dominant social practice of seeing male and female in a hierarchical relationship wherein the male is superior and the female inferior. Ruether acknowledges Kari Børreson's important study, *Subordination and Equivalence in Nature: The Nature and Role of Women in Augustine and Thomas Aquinas*. Elizabeth Clark and Herbert Richardson have compiled primary texts representing both points of view in *Women and Religion: A Feminist Sourcebook of Christian Thought*. See also Margaret Farley's "Sources of Sexual Inequality in the History of Christian Thought."

For studies in other religious traditions, see Arvind Sharma, ed., *Women in World Religions*. Rita M. Gross, for example, uncovers analogous views and practices in the tribal religions of aboriginal Australia and elucidates their complexities according to the themes of *exclusion* and *participation* (37–58).

9. My article "Rereading, Reconceiving, and Reconstructing Traditions: Feminist Research in Religion" discusses a variety of tasks that characterizes current research on women and religion (1980–) and relates these to specific sources pertaining to a variety of traditions (cross-cultural studies, goddess studies, studies in Judaism, Christianity, Islam, Hinduism, Buddhism, Native American, African American and African traditional religions, contemporary religious ethics, and the like).

10. For many, the goal of feminist research is not limited to academic inquiry or historical investigation, but includes institutional and social change. Rosemary Ruether has made this point in an illustrative metaphor: "We are contending, not simply for a part of the pie, but for a new way of baking the pie itself, even to rewriting the basic recipe" (75th Anniversary Lecture, American Academy of Religion annual meeting, 1984; published as "The Future of Feminist Theology in the Academy," 712).

"hermeneutic of suspicion"[11] to inherited moral theory that traditionally has been constructed by men. Since religious ethical norms, axioms, ideals, and rules represent the collective wisdom of the human community as digested and articulated by mostly male creators and shapers of tradition, feminist religious ethicists wish to take a new look at those conclusions and reconsider them in light of women's experiences, interpretations, and judgments. To do so is not to jettison received theories, but rather to work to extend the "data base," to expand the range of resources used, so that an ever fuller expression of life serves as the backdrop for an assessment of those theories, functioning in a supportive or critical-corrective manner.

Feminist religious ethics takes women's experiences seriously as a starting point and wishes to stay focused on women's experiences in addition to men's experiences as a central source of insight. My own hope, as one feminist interested in religion and ethics, is that this line of inquiry will feed and broaden the streams of experience upon which theory is based. Each of us must say what we see and what we think of what we see. As voices of all kind join this enterprise—women's and men's voices, the educated elites and the broader populations of the less educated and uneducated, the rich and the poor, people of various cultural, racial, class, and geographic background—the hope is that our theory-making efforts will more adequately represent the broad array of human experience, vision, and judgment, and therefore be more accurate and useful.

This study focuses on one woman. In writing it I hope to illuminate the writings, thoughts, arguments, sensibilities, aspirations, judgments, choices, actions, and person of Dorothy Day by bringing to her writings a variety of questions stimulated by recent research on women. At the same time, I hope to address and enrich current efforts to construct feminist theory in general and feminist religious ethics more specifically by feeding into that process the views of one particularly interesting twentieth-century woman. My sources are the public writings by and about Dorothy Day and recorded interviews with her. A number of historical studies pertaining to both Day and the Catholic Worker movement make it possible and timely to focus a study on her moral vision and moral praxis from a feminist perspective.[12]

---

11. Paul Ricoeur, *Hermeneutics and the Human Sciences*; Elisabeth Schüssler Fiorenza, *In Memory of Her*; Juan Luis Segundo, *The Liberation of Theology*.
12. Historical studies that ground this study in feminist religious ethics are William A. Au, *The Cross, the Flag, and the Bomb*; Brigid O'Shea Merriman, "Searching for Christ"; William Miller, *Dorothy Day* and *A Harsh and Dreadful Love*; Mel Piehl, *Breaking Bread*; Nancy Roberts, *Dorothy Day and the Catholic Worker*. While not a

I am interested at the outset in the ways in which Dorothy Day saw herself. Chapter one takes seriously her self-understanding as writer, for Day was a person who wrote from an early age, enjoyed writing, and came to see writing as her vocation. Chapters two through four probe three other self-images that emerge with force: woman, religious convert, and radical. In each chapter, questions with a feminist interest serve to illuminate Day's thought and praxis; conversely, Day's thinking is sought as one resource that might offer insight to current questions and debates in feminist religious ethics. Chapter five is written to examine Day precisely as moralist. Although she does not use the word *moralist* to describe herself, the moral passion and intensity together with the moral beliefs and concerns that pervade her understandings and activities justify this label. Her entire working life was an effort "to arouse the conscience," a phrase she picked up from her co-Worker, Peter Maurin. It is a phrase, however, that aptly describes her pre-Maurin period as well as her work with Maurin. For she had sought to arouse the conscience of her readers as a radical journalist before she met Maurin as well as during her work with him as a radical Christian. Chapter five highlights the religio-ethical norms that Dorothy Day derived from her experience as writer, woman, religious, and radical, and notes the ways in which she, as a twentieth-century American woman, with Anglo-Saxon and middle-class roots, understood and approached the moral life.

Dorothy Day has aroused strong emotions, both supportive and critical. She has been described as a modern saint, as the most interesting and important person in American Catholicism, as one of the great figures of the twentieth century, as a person of the stature of Mohandas Gandhi and Martin Luther King, Jr.[13] Others, by contrast, have asserted that her pacifist position was unrealistic and that as an agent of social change Dorothy Day was misguided and ineffective. The claim is made that although feeding the poor who came to the soup kitchens was admirable, Day's efforts functioned, in fact, as mere palliatives for the few and had no impact on the unjust social system through which large numbers of people are systematically and continuously marginalized and outcast.[14]

---

historical study as historians define the term, this ethical inquiry is rooted in historical documents and historical studies. Good ethics takes seriously the work of historians and other scholars whose work includes the assertion, documentation, and interpretation of facts which ethicists relate to questions of value.

13. Nancy Roberts, *Dorothy Day and the Catholic Worker*, 4–5, quoting historian David J. O'Brien; Linda Bamber in the *Nation*; Gary Wills, syndicated columnist; and Petra Kelly, leader of West Germany's Green party.

14. Paul Hanly Furfey, *Love and the Urban Ghetto*, 111–30.

Since the purpose of my book is at once expository and interpretive, the tone may seem detached in comparison with the impassioned claims made by Day's admirers and critics. It is my hope that my nonimpassioned tone will better enable readers to discover the contour and content of Dorothy Day's moral vision and, especially important to me, to reckon with it on their own.

1

THE WRITER: AUTOBIOGRAPHER, DIARIST, REPORTER

DOROTHY DAY IS WIDELY KNOWN as a social critic, protestor, and dissenter, as anarchist, pacifist, and Communist become Catholic, as advocacy journalist and editor of *The Catholic Worker* newspaper, as founder of numerous houses of hospitality for the homeless, as single parent, working mother, and grandmother. Some would add to this list the label saint. Given the international recognition and notoriety which Day has received, I wonder how the labels by others relate to Day's own personal sense of self. For example, which, if any, of her many public identities resonated most deeply within her? What categories, images, and descriptions did she select to describe and present herself to her readers? How did these take expression in her writings and why were they important to her? Since one of the most fundamental of ethical questions is "what kind of person do I want to become?" (its collective form being "what kind of people do we want to be?" or "what kind of society do we want to create?"), the forms Day selected and the reflections she offered are important clues for gaining insight into her ethic.

As an adult whose income depended on her writing, Day practiced her conviction that she could only write from experience because she could only know that which she had experienced. Thus all of her works are personal by design, deliberately autobiographical in tone and intent. Although she described herself at one point as "a journalist and a diarist pure and simple," rather than a writer of books, she admitted that as long as she could remember, she had dreamed of writing novels (LL, 183).[1] Even the one novel she did write was admittedly autobiographical.[2]

Recent studies about women's autobiographies raise the question of whether a distinctive tradition of women's autobiography might be differentiated from a tradition of male-authored autobiographies.[3] Given the traditionally disparate social worlds in which men and women have lived their lives, learned their roles, and expressed their responsibilities, it seems plausible that their autobiographical forms, styles, and emphases might indeed be notably distinct. Estelle Jelinek observes that the female tradition in autobiography emphasizes the personal over the historical and family life over career, and that it is expressed in a disjunctiveness of forms rather than in the progressive narratives[4] that characterize men's autobiographies. This hypothesis provides an additional set of questions I find intriguing as I examine Dorothy Day's self-perceptions and self-presentations. Did she place the accent on the "personal" or the "historical," on "family life" or "career"? Are her narratives "disjunctive," employing a multitude of genres or "progressive," that is, literarily unified in form? If there is a distinctively female autobiographical tradition, does Dorothy Day stand within it, or outside it, I wonder, or perhaps move in and out of

---

1. Textual citations from Day's books are as follows: *The Eleventh Virgin* (EV), *From Union Square to Rome* (US), *House of Hospitality* (HH), *Loaves and Fishes* (LF), *The Long Loneliness* (LL), *Meditations* (M), *On Pilgrimage* (OP), *On Pilgrimage: The Sixties* (OPS); also the Robert Ellsberg edition of Day's selected writings, *By Little and By Little* (BL).

2. William Miller, *Dorothy Day: A Biography*, 5, 123; Miller, *All Is Grace*, 2; Robert Coles, *Dorothy Day: A Radical Devotion*, 36–37.

3. Estelle Jelinek, *Women's Autobiography: Essays in Criticism* and *The Tradition of Women's Autobiography: From Antiquity to the Present*. See also Sidonie Smith, *A Poetics of Women's Autobiography*, and Mary Mason, "The Other Voice: Autobiographies of Women Writers," in James Olney, ed., *Autobiography: Essays Theoretical and Critical*.

4. "Rather than the progressive, linear, unidimensional works that men wrote—chronicles, *res gestae*, intellectual histories—most women's self-portraits are cast in discontinuous forms and disjunctive narratives. Diaries, letters, and journals . . . are accessible forms for women whose emotional, intellectual, and practical lives are fragmented by domestic responsibilities that leave them little leisure time to contemplate or integrate their experiences. Even in more shaped narratives and autobiographies proper, a disjunctiveness persists. Although the women attempt to maintain some chronology, to show some progression in their lives, they interrupt their narratives with anecdotes, character sketches, lectures, letters, and flashbacks—no matter what the subject matter, from Indian captivity to reform movements" (Jelinek, *Tradition*, 104; see also 33).

both men's and women's autobiographical styles? Or does her work provide cause for altering these interpretive categories?

As a member of a family of newspaper writers, Dorothy Day had been taught early to write personally and subjectively about what she saw and what was being done (LF, 7). She kept a diary as a child even at the risk of her brothers finding it and taunting her about it, because in writing she found comfort: "Recording happiness made it last longer, we felt, and recording sorrow dramatized it and took away its bitterness; and often we settled some problem which beset us even while we wrote about it" (US, 110; see also LL, 132).

As a self-supporting adult, Day chose to be a journalist because writing was her "talent," her interest, her way to pay the bills; she came to see it also as her "vocation" (OP, 174–75; US, 173; LL, 109; LF, 86). Indeed, when she met Peter Maurin, her mentor and co-founder of the Catholic Worker, what most caught her attention and fired her imagination was his idea of establishing a labor newspaper (HH, xxvii; LF, 7). Her purposes in writing were many: to make known the experiences of the inarticulate, to spotlight the cracks in the social system, and to disclose human suffering so that action might be taken to prevent and alleviate it; to discuss and clarify ideas about how to improve the social order and to argue on behalf of the values of anarchism, voluntary poverty, and pacifism in contrast to prevailing social and cultural preferences for institutionalized expressions of power, materialism, and militarism. She described herself as an "editor of a monthly paper, presenting a point of view about what is going on in the world," "vital happenings," "matters of life and death" (OPS, 75). These included wars (the Japanese-Chinese War, the Ethiopian War, Spanish Civil War, World War II and the Korean war, and later, the war in Vietnam), labor strikes (on streetcars, in garment factories, sugar refineries, and smelting plants [US, 69]), and policies of conscription.

Because Day's journalistic writings were intended to reflect and to serve direct action, the bulk of her works—including whole books—were written between activities, often as fragments. No attempt was made to cast her prose in elegant style (M, 4). Yet she loved to write and mused in one entry that in light of all the pages given to ideas, theories, and efforts to understand, she found relief and relaxation in just writing about facts, in simply giving an account of her day (OP, 134).

As Day's writings gain wider attention, her autobiographical novel, *The Eleventh Virgin*, invites examination along with her journals, essays, editorials, and other books. Written in her mid-twenties, *The Eleventh Virgin* provides insight into the early Dorothy Day, before she became religiously impelled, before she met Peter Maurin, before she founded the Catholic Worker. *The Eleventh Virgin* portrays the adolescence of the protagonist June, daughter, sister, and playmate; child who experiences an awakening sexuality; young woman student, friend, reporter, and nurse; passionate lover and rejected lover who tastes the enjoyment and delight of intimacy, yet knows also manipulation, humiliation, and abandonment; a woman who elects an abortion, yet in its midst sustains a lively hope for marriage and babies.

Written at age forty, *From Union Square to Rome* is Day's account of her journey to religious faith and thus is written to explain to her brother and other Communist friends and relatives why she moved from a publicly expressed empathy for communism to a commitment to Catholic Christianity. In this book, Day put the spotlight on her mind and heart, articulating the questions that bothered her, the values that attracted her, the religious interests that haunted her, the vices that diminished her, the decisions she felt were required of her. A well-crafted book, *From Union Square to Rome* not only voices her story but also makes public a rationale for her conversion. *The Long Loneliness: The Autobiography of Dorothy Day* (1952) continues, at times repeats, this conversion story, and though cast in the genre of autobiography, receives a disclaimer by its author. "I have never intended to write an autobiography," Day wrote. "I have always wanted instead to tell of things that brought me to God and that reminded me of God" (LL, 110; see also US, ix). This intention enabled Day to omit those elements of her life that she felt led her away from God, details included in her novel which was written well in advance of her conversion. *Loaves and Fishes* provides Day's portrait of the Catholic Worker. Taken together, these four books can be construed as a four-volume autobiography, for all are autobiographical in both substance and style. Seen together, they enlarge the autobiographical lens by which we are able to see Dorothy Day in her multiple identities and thus answer questions about her self-understandings and moral sensibilities. In distinctively different ways, each lends insight into Dorothy Day's moral concerns, convictions, and commitments.

The Eleventh Virgin gained movie rights for Day, paying her and her publisher five thousand dollars. A movie was never made and the book fell into literary oblivion. It is no longer in print. An unnamed *New York Times* book reviewer faulted the novel on several counts, claiming that it lacked proper "adherence to form" and "arrangement" and that it bespoke an eagerness to speak the truth of adolescence without sufficient concern for effectively structuring and artistically patterning that truth. The same reviewer who rightly critiqued the book on literary grounds, however, praised *The Eleventh Virgin* as being a novel with notable insight into modern life, "written with understanding and feeling" and marked by "some very good writing" about "striking and interesting incidents culled from the lives of an attractive group of people."[5]

Day herself became a harsh critic of the book. More than a decade after its publication, she described *The Eleventh Virgin* as "a very bad book" (US, 109). The protagonist June's youthful sexual liaisons, the abortion she underwent in a private apartment, and her general sense of being adrift in life, undoubtedly conveyed sad memories to an older, less mercurial Dorothy. The book became more than a source of sadness and personal embarrassment to its converted Catholic author, however; it became also a source of anxiety and even a preoccupation for a time. Decades after its publication, Dorothy Day told an interviewer,

> There was a time that I thought I had a lifetime job cut out for me—to track down every copy of that novel and destroy them all, one by one. . . . I used to lie in bed thinking about the book in all the libraries, and once I even tried to find out how many libraries there are in the country. I knew, of course, that most of them had better things to do with their funds than buy a novel from an unknown writer, but the book was in a few libraries, and my hope was to get rid of it as completely as I could.[6]

Dorothy later labeled this wish "the sin of pride, if there ever was an example of it," resigning herself to accept the book, while adding, "I still hope that no one who hasn't read it ever will."[7] This book provides glimpses into a Dorothy Day that she preferred to forget and to have us never know.

Dedicated to three unnamed friends, and, curiously enough, to herself ("to H.N., to J.K., to a girl whose initials I cannot remember, and although it is not customary to include oneself in dedications, to myself"), *The Eleventh Virgin* is cast in three parts: Part One, "Adolescent," Part Two, "Still Adolescent," and Part Three, "Not So Much So." Several commonly acknowledged features of adolescence give direction to the story: the excitement of discovery, ambivalence in selecting a personal creed, a desire for conversation together with a

---

5. "Truth Incoherent," *New York Times*, 27 April 1924, III, 95.
6. Coles, *Radical Devotion*, 37. This work is based on notes from years of conversation with Day and on tape-recorded interviews over a two-year period in the early 1970s.
7. Coles, *Radical Dveotion*, 37, 38.

recurrent sense of its futility, and a vivid fantasy life. A detailed sum-
mary of the story is necessary at this point for understanding Day's
early experience and subsequent writings.

An awakening sensuality and occasional glimpses into spirituality
characterize the protagonist June's early discoveries and stimulate fan-
tasies charged with a sense of mystery. With respect to things sexual,
she became aware of "life's secrets" (EV, 8) from a girlfriend, Sadie, and
she sensed an exciting wickedness about this knowledge. At the age of
eight, she was hugged and kissed by Harvey, a fourteen-year-old neighbor, and found this all very thrilling. With respect to things spiritual,
June learned something about "the mysteries" (EV, 16) of religion from
another friend, Mary, who provided June with a book about a saint. For
a time, June and her sister Adele sought to emulate the asceticism of the
saints by transforming their bedroom into a bare cell and sleeping on
the floor. This brief experiment in spirituality provoked a period of
inquiry. June became bothered by the "question of her soul and where
she was before she was born and what would become of her afterward"
(EV, 18).

Such questions led her to read Herbert Spencer, Immanuel Kant,
and Baruch Spinoza, whom she found incomprehensible, but also
Edgar Allan Poe and Charles Darwin, whom she could understand, and
authors on ancient religion. An interest in the Episcopal Church
awakened, though June found church services disappointing. She came
to know "the pleasurable conviction of sin" (EV, 19) not through
religion but by falling in love, which yielded for June a sense of whole-
ness, a feeling of body-mind integration that she had not known before.
She found it "strange and wonderful that a thought, a glance, could
make a little shiver of delight run through her" (EV, 23). As one who
"loved to be bitten by fierce emotion" (EV, 28), June had plenty of such
emotion in a short-lived but richly fantasized love for Mr. Armand, the
band director for the neighborhood park summer concerts. When this
summer fantasy ended as fall began, June searched elsewhere for meaning and satisfaction. She found some interest in the Bible, but it took the
writings of John Wesley, Jonathan Edwards, and Thomas à Kempis to
evoke her religious enthusiasm.

June's friend, Henrietta, provided June an outlet for an increasingly
introspective spirit. It was to Henrietta that June voiced a desire for
spiritual happiness and a sense of conflict between the self as sensual
and the divine as spiritual. Her empathy for spiritual matters and
spiritual disciplines, however, remained superficial and June admitted
to her sister Adele, as she was growing tired of religion, that her
religious expressions were no more than a pose. Yet she redeemed this

confession with a question: "didn't everyone have poses, and why was one more objectionable than another?" (EV, 43)

In the course of her college years, June joined in coffee house debates about men and women's differing approaches to sexuality and marriage, childbearing, and childrearing. June's mind served as the forum for a debate on sexuality when she was eighteen. Two friends battle it out within her. Billy, an artist, regarded sex as a barrier that needed to be broken down in order for complete freedom between the sexes to be possible. Billy regarded love affairs as incidents in the erotic education of a woman which made her more lovable rather than less because of all that the experienced woman was capable of teaching the man she loved. Ellen, on the other hand, held women's virginity in high esteem; purity of body enabled purity of mind. Men preferred pure women; they "don't want to be taught, they want to teach" (EV, 122). Billy and Ellen fought it out in June's mind. Only eighteen, uncertain what she believed and not yet ready to formulate a creed for herself, June listened to each side, remaining ambivalent. It would be several years (and many pages in the novel) before she would make a choice — in Billy's direction.

June's interest in social issues was heightened during her college years. She and her friends debated a variety of issues: whether free verse was poetry, whether capitalists did more harm than good, whether state control had ever been successful, whether the brotherhood of man was a real possibility. These interests led her to become a reporter for the socialist press after college. Her low pay challenged her to live frugally and provided an avenue for understanding and reporting on life in the tenements of New York. She also covered stories about birth control, women in prison, and prostitution. She marched on behalf of the suffragists (as political prisoners, not as suffragists) and was briefly imprisoned in the process. The jail experience seemed to her an experience of uselessness just as many of her earlier conversations (about sexuality, about differing attitudes among men and women, about various social causes) had generated a sense of futility (EV, 56, 138, 207, 270).

June's desire to do something in life that would be both simple and useful was awakened in prison. This desire found expression in nursing when journalism opportunities were in short supply and when nurses were needed during wartime. In her nursing work, June met Dick, an orderly at the hospital, whom she came to love and with whom she lived and became pregnant. The relationship was marked by Dick's desire to have June wait on him and be dependent in such a way as to sit at home and think of him all day, having no other interests than being his. June's reflections on these expectations are that it is "delightfully humiliating" (EV, 278) to be talked to in these terms. She cooperated fully, spending her days reading and dreaming in his apartment. Not unaware of the choices she was making, June wondered at one point: "Why was it that women idolized men that scorned them?" (EV, 285) Dick was clear about the vacillating, temporary and possessive nature of his love, describing love itself at one point as simply a "very wearing emotion" (EV, 296). When she learned she was pregnant, June felt pressed to seek an abortion, endured it alone without Dick's presence or support, and recognized that she had brought this misery upon herself. She recognized that she had "loved him for his irresponsibility—for the happy-go-lucky way he slid through life" (EV, 300). Part Three of *The Eleventh Virgin* concludes with June's discovery of a farewell note from Dick. He had left for new work that required relocation and he used a letter to end their intimacy. When he sees her again (presumably several years later), he writes, he hopes she will be married to a rich man so that he might borrow money from her. The next day, June received a poem from Dick urging her to recognize the ultimate unimportance of their feelings for each other in the larger scheme of things and to forget him.

A rather anticlimactic and contrived monologue, attached to Part Three, concludes the novel. In it, June offers Adele random thoughts. Central among them are these: " . . . I fell in love, happily at an early age, and I'm still in love . . . I know what I want. It's Dick and marriage and babies! And I'll have them yet. Wait and see" (EV, 312). Thus, at novel's end, June appears to be stuck in her adolescent fantasy life, even though the title of Part Three ("Not So Much So") would seem to intimate growth into greater wisdom. June had achieved some level of introspection and recognition of herself as the cause of her problems with Dick, yet she clung to her desire and created from that desire an ungrounded hope for marriage to him and babies with him. She recognized that she was attracted to irresponsibility in men. She is thus not a tragic figure but rather a foolish figure, for she self-consciously nourished a relationship that did not and could not meet her own goals or needs and gave no evidence of having benefited Dick either. June's creator and historical counterpart had reason to feel embarrassed about *The Eleventh Virgin* as autobiographical novel, it would seem, on grounds of June's sheer immaturity, independently of Dorothy's changed judgments about meaning and morality. At novel's end, June, an adult working woman, remained a willing participant in a stunting adolescent fantasy.

Day had harsh words about this period in her life. At forty, she alluded to "my early twenties when I, too, was tasting the bitterness and the dregs of life and shuddered at its harshness and cruelty" (US, 8). She came to view this as a time when she was "floundering," "undisciplined," and "amoral" (US, 127), "intoxicated" by her freedom: "I felt a sense of reckless arrogance and with this recklessness, I felt a sense of danger and rejoiced in it. It was good to live dangerously" (US, 45). She viewed her youthful stance as "arrogant," "pathetic, little, and mean in its very excuse for itself" (US, 2). William Miller's biography of Day reconstructs those years, offering historical facts about Day's relationship ("affair") with Lionel Moise ("Dick" in EV) and her one year marriage to Barkeley Tobey (which Day later felt she had entered into unfairly, on the rebound from Moise) together with her intimate and live-in relationship with Forster Batterham, lover to Dorothy and father to their daughter, Tamar.[8] Day, the social critic, turned the criticism on herself in a book that is an apologia in the classic sense, *From Union Square to Rome* (1938).

Union Square, Day's explanation and account of her shift from belief in communism to faith in Christianity, was written to answer the question voiced by communist friends and relatives, "How could you become a Catholic?"[9] It was written also for Catholics who regarded her as "an enemy boring from within" (US, ix). Day's personal style of writing is particularly pronounced through use of the second person form, as in a letter. This is a consciously shaped and artistically structured work of thirteen chapters in which she surveyed her past with an eye well-focused on her communist sympathies, offering explanation and insight about why communism did not sustain those sympathies in the long run. Eleven of the thirteen chapters are primarily narrative in form and include journal entries from her past. Chapters twelve and thirteen resemble essays in theological apologetics: one addresses three fundamental beliefs of communism (materialism, communal ownership, and the necessity for violent means of social change); the other responds to three objections to religion (religion is morbid, the Catholic liturgy has a cannibalistic aspect that is revolting, and Christianity fails

---

8. Although Dorothy regularly described her relationship with Batterham as a "common-law marriage," she noted that Forster, who did not believe in marriage, "never allowed me to forget that this was a comradeship rather than a marriage" (LL, 137). Nonetheless, Dorothy continued to refer to Forster as her "husband" throughout her life, "even after a half-century's separation" (Jim Forest, *Love Is the Measure*, 201).

9. Day had been baptized on 29 December 1927 in Our Lady Help of Christians Church in Tottenville, Staten Island. For dates pertaining to Day, I rely on Brigid Merriman's historical study "Searching for Christ." Dorothy Day herself was not always accurate in her dating, and Miller, her biographer, does not always correct her. See Merriman, 367, n. 27, 370, n. 24, and 416–17, n. 23.

to account for the existence and cause of evil in its claims that God is Creator of all things). Day's intent and purpose are explicit:

> . . . what I want to bring out in this book is a succession of events that led me to His feet, glimpses of Him that I received through many years which made me feel the vital need of Him and of religion. I will try to trace for you the steps by which I came to accept the faith that I believe was always in my heart. [US, 1]

The sharpness and clarity of purpose, however, did not dim this writer's awareness that though she feared avoiding the truth or distorting it, she could not fully prevent either, for she wrote of a past which brought with it a radical change of perspective. Thus she admitted, "when I look for causes of my conversion, sometimes it is one thing and sometimes it is another that stands out in my mind" (US, 3).

With this and similar statements, the book reflects the self-consciousness of the writer acutely aware of the way a shift in standpoint alters perspective. Autobiographical writing is now widely recognized to reflect both artistry and history.[10] It is both construct and record. The autobiographer records and narrates, creates and constructs, using this form, that selection, this framework, that image to render into a unified and coherent view a multiplicity of moments, persons, places, events, and influences.

From a consciously embraced Christian social standpoint, Day rethought her life, recounting her positive feelings, for example, when as a child she read the Bible in an attic with her sister. Having grown up in a family where God was never mentioned, this sense of discovering God brought with it rich, deep, and full feelings. Yet they were feelings that could not be sustained and a shift in feeling moved a disillusioned young Dorothy to wonder whether religion was merely reducible to a game or analogous to a garment (US, 22). Though she continued to believe in God and read the Bible intermittently, she stopped attending church. In college she came to agree with a professor that religion was a prop which the strong did not need; she consciously and deliberately turned from religion as from an opiate (US, 41–42).

Day's critical view toward religion was also influenced by the dramatic need for justice. She found the saints impressive yet wondered

---

10. See, for example, Jelinek, Smith, Mason, and Olney, cited in n. 3 above; also John Morris, *Versions of the Self*, William Spengemann, *The Forms of Autobiography: Episodes in the History of a Literary Genre*, William Zinsser, *Inventing the Truth: The Art and Craft of Memoir*, and Janet Varner Gunn, *Autobiography: Toward a Poetics of Experience*.

why so much love was spent in remedying evil rather than finding ways to prevent it; she felt they should not just minister to slaves but work to do away with slavery (US, 47). Yet again and again she felt prodded to recognize God as her first beginning and last end (US, 88). This recognition was stimulated by her reading, her social protest, and her experience of nature. Tolstoy, Dostoyevsky, and Francis Thompson were favorites. She favored Tolstoy's view of Christianity without church or priesthood (US, 81) and she loved Thompson's poem, *The Hound of Heaven* (which Eugene O'Neill first recited to her "in the back room of a saloon on Sixth Avenue" [US, 7]), describing it as "one of those poems that awakens the soul, recalls to it the fact that God is its destiny" (US, 88).

Day's religious sensibilities were consonant with her social action involvements. Yet her empathy for workers initially pulled her in many directions simultaneously, and at the age of eighteen she wavered in allegiance to socialism, syndicalism (the I.W.W.'s), and anarchism (US, 68). She exulted in the victory of the 1917 Russian Revolution and, as a reporter for *The Call*, she worked from noon to midnight covering picket lines, starvation, and death in New York's slums. As a worker for the Anti-Conscription League, she sought to persuade people not to register for the draft (US, 78). She had found strength in the words of Eugene Debs which moved her to become involved in a variety of social activities: "While there is a lower class, I am of it, and while there is a criminal element, I am of it, and while there is a soul in prison, I am not free" (US, 102). She was thus poised later to find meaning in the Catholic doctrine of the Mystical Body of Christ, a metaphor expressing the interdependence of people with one another and with God symbolized as members of the one body of Christ (US, 140). Reviewing her life led her to the realization that religious faith had had a longer history in her soul than had her radical sympathies.

> . . . long before I became a radical I had felt deeply the mysteries of faith, not *the* Faith, but faith nevertheless. Remember, I read the Bible when I was twelve, and I knew what my conscience was, and what was good and evil. I had accepted the doctrine of the Holy Eucharist. So when I came back to God there was not that difficulty to overcome. [US, 159]

Apparently the return was neither easy nor smooth. "No one but God knows how long I struggled, how I turned to Him, and turned from Him, again and again" (US, 157).

Pregnancy and the birth of her daughter Tamar in March of 1926

had powerfully alerted Day to the wonders of creation which she felt led
her to the source of creation, awakening her faith in God: "Human love
at its best, unselfish, glowing, illuminating our days, gives us a glimpse
of the love of God for man" (US, 151). This sense of God's love
convinced Dorothy that she would have Tamar baptized and be baptized herself even though this choice would require separation from her
common-law husband, the baby's father, who could not accept her
religious interests. Day deliberately sketched this part of her life in
Union Square, admitting "These pages are hard to write. The struggle
was too personal. It was exceedingly difficult" (US, 141). It would be
fourteen years later before Day would detail her love for and separation
from Forster Batterham. That story is told with power and feeling in
The Long Loneliness.

The Long Loneliness: The Autobiography of Dorothy Day (1952) is
a more comprehensive story of her life than is *Union Square*, but again
one notes a focused interest on religious influences. Three disclaimers
punctuate the narrative: (1) "I have never intended to write an autobiography. I have always wanted instead to tell of things that brought me
to God and that reminded me of God" (LL, 110). (2) "I am a journalist,
not a biographer, not a *book* writer. The sustained effort of writing, of
putting pen to paper so many hours a day when there are human beings
around who need me, when there is sickness, and hunger, and sorrow, is
a harrowingly painful job" (LL, 9). (3) "I do not want to write about
other people with whom I was intimately associated" (LL, 110) or
about people whose privacy requires silence. Thus we are warned by
the author of several limitations to her narrative: limits in intention,
limits in capacity, limits imposed by her respect for the privacy of
others.

A brief reflection on the twofold meaning of confession as acknowl-
edgment of one's sins and as autobiography opens the narrative. Three
additional sections comprise the bulk of the book: Part One, "Searching," spans the first twenty-five years of Day's life, years detailed in *The
Eleventh Virgin* and events surrounding its publication and payment of
revenues. Part Two, "Natural Happiness," describes her relationship
with Forster Batterham, the birth of her daughter Tamar, her conversion to and baptism in the Catholic church, the separation from
Forster, and her meeting Peter Maurin. Part Three, "Love Is the Measure," tells about how and why Peter impressed her and offers some
details about the growth of the Catholic Worker movement.

Central events that mark this life story are familiar to readers of
The Eleventh Virgin. Passages encountered in *Union Square* are met
again in *The Long Loneliness*, sometimes in identical form, suggesting

direct copying from one book to another or the use of a common source such as a journal entry written at an earlier time.[11] *The Long Loneliness*, unlike *The Eleventh Virgin*, enabled Day to become analytical as well as expository in her writing, observing and assessing her experience, reflecting on its implications and envisioning alternatives.[12] One example:

> There was never any kissing in my family, and never a close embrace. There was only a firm, austere kiss from my mother every night. My sister and I took out our desire for physical expression of affection on our baby brother. We kept ourselves to ourselves, as the saying is, but I don't see any particular virtue in that attitude. It is the way we were as a family; and we were like most Anglo-Saxons. It made us, I am sure, more intense, more sensual, more conscious of the flesh which we continually denied. We could never be free with others, never put our arms around them casually, lean against others companionably as I see Italian boys doing in this neighborhood where we live. We were never handholders. We were always withdrawn and alone, unlike Italians, Poles, Jews, and other friends I had who were fresh and spontaneous in their affection. [LL, 39–40]

The themes of aloneness and loneliness recur. Day often felt alone as a child in spite of having had two brothers and a sister. She found joy in being alone and detailed her solitary play time in the garden, with dolls, making perfume from flower petals, watching anthills (LL, 19). As an adult, this recurring sense of aloneness became a source of pain rather than joy (LL, 57, 58, 179, 180). Undoubtedly it enhanced her ability to recognize loneliness in others (LL, 272, 318, 227) and to seek to alleviate their pain by nurturing community.

The childhood experience of neighborly community wherein everyone helped one another after the San Francisco earthquake of 1906 served as a memory with driving force. Day's native empathy for the

---

11. See, for example, US, 110–11 and LL, 132; US, 122 and LL, 151; US, 126 and LL, 153; US, 127 and LL, 155; US, 132 and LL, 157.

12. James Olney writes about this feature of autobiographical writing more generally: "autobiography is a self-reflexive, a self-critical act, and consequently the criticism of autobiography exists *within* the literature instead of alongside it. . . . This is markedly different from the constraints . . . under which the novelist operates. Certainly the novelist can comment on, theorize about, analyze and criticize his fiction if he so desires—but he must go outside the work to do it" (and thereby surrender a large part of his status as creator). See "Autobiography and the Cultural Moment: A Thematic, Historical, and Bibliographical Introduction," in James Olney, ed., *Autobiography*, 25.

destitute was later stimulated and deepened by the writings of Eugene Debs, Peter Kropotkin, Jack London, and Upton Sinclair, readings she began as early as age fourteen. Appalled by the poverty she witnessed as a twenty-year-old reporter in New York, she nevertheless felt attracted to that setting: "as I walked these streets back in 1917 I wanted to go and live among these surroundings; in some mysterious way I felt that I would never be freed from this burden of loneliness and sorrow unless I did" (LL, 58).

This inclination, combined with the revolutionary consciousness abroad at the time, led Day to align with the (literary and liberal segment of) the radical movement: Max Eastman and Floyd Dell (editors of the *Masses*), Eugene O'Neill, Michael Gold, Hart Crane (LL, 78, 95, 129). Having rejected religion during her university years as an opiate and having criticized religious people as tepid and materialistic (LL, 48, 71), Day began going to church at this time, drawn partly by the large numbers of churchgoing poor for whom she felt, wrote, and marched.

Two relationships shaped Day's subsequent story: her love relationship with Forster Batterham and her working relationship with Peter Maurin. The differences Dorothy sensed between herself and Forster and herself and Peter are as important as are the attractions, for differences test and disclose commitment. While Dorothy and Forster both felt strongly about injustice, for example, their differences dwarfed this common concern. Whereas Dorothy was moved to do something about the injustices she saw (voice them in her reports, be with those who suffered), Forster tended to handle his sadness by withdrawing into solitude. Whereas Dorothy loved conversation and community, longed for marriage and children, and was drawn to religion, Forster was quiet, given to individualism, unwilling to marry, reluctant to parent, and outraged by religion.

Peter Maurin shared Dorothy's commitments to community and a Christian social vision, yet their differences were equally pronounced. Peter accepted these with the help of a quip: "man proposes and woman disposes" (LL, 199). Dorothy provided a fuller explanation, having recognized a number of significant differences. Peter was French, she American; he was twenty years older than she, from a family of peasants who loved and lived close to the land, whereas she was a product of the city and one who loved living in the city. When he spoke about workers, he thought of farmers, builders, machine and tool-makers, while when she spoke about workers, she pictured factories, the proletariat, the slum dwellers, and the unemployed. Where he had lived alone as an itinerant for much of his life, she found life with others in community to be vital to her spirit and her source of joy and hope (LL, 199–200, also 205). She wrote about conditions; he about ideals.[13]

As much as she loved Forster and respected Peter, Dorothy was a strong-willed, forceful person who stood her ground, made judgments according to her lights and saw these through to action, even as these actions generated unwanted conflict. Her "comradeship" (LL, 137) with Forster was loving but short-lived and their sharp differences were handled by separation. With respect to Peter, Dorothy quickly recognized the need for her leadership if the newspaper venture would be successful: she chose the press, used her earnings for printing costs, determined the price (one cent per copy to make it affordable to anyone who wanted to read it), selected and placed the entries, and insisted on her title "The Catholic Worker" rather than his "The Catholic Radical" (LL, 199). Peter's statement of aims was not even the lead editorial in the first issue of 1 May 1933 (LF, 22). Furthermore, Peter never participated in the work of the paper, except to submit a half dozen of his easy essays each month, many of which he insisted be repeated over and over again.[14] Nor did he ever personally serve the breadline or join Day in strike activities. ("Strikes don't strike me," he quipped [LF, 21].) Not known for possessing a sense of efficiency (LF, 95), Maurin nevertheless did tend to tasks around the house such as "mending chairs with bits of wire, building fires, carrying out ashes."[15] Often he would leave for days or weeks as a time, neither leaving nor sending word as to his whereabouts.[16]

Yet Dorothy discovered important things from both. From her life with Forster (1924–27) she had learned to enjoy being alone at the beach, digging for clams, collecting shells. With Peter (1932–49) she had come to appreciate a sense of history and a vision that could sustain her even as she gave herself to the immediacy of the moment, publishing a paper and otherwise meeting people's needs. Forster had stretched her into the world of biology and nature, Peter into the world of theology and history.

While Dorothy's associations and friendships with women received regular mention (Peggy Baird, her sister Della, Nina Polcyn, Eileen Egan, among others), no single woman friend nor community of women friends received special attention in the way Forster or Peter did. Dorothy seems to have lived in a primarily male world, both as a radical

---

13. Dorothy Day, "I Remember Peter Maurin," 36.
14. Day, "I Remember Peter Maurin," 36.
15. Day, "I Remember Peter Maurin," 39.
16. Marc Ellis, *Peter Maurin*, 132–38.

reporter and, later, as a radical Christian and editor. Her story is notable for its dearth of discussion about living female role models, friends, or confidants. She conveyed deep and continuous affection for her mother and her sister Della with whom she kept in contact, but neither seems to have had a major impact on Dorothy's thinking, values, or spiritual interests and commitments. She was critical of the suffragists, critical of the women who would most likely use the vote once it was won, critical of Emma Goldman, critical also of Sister Aloysia, the Catholic nun whom Dorothy spoke to on the Staten Island beaches as she clarified her desire to have Tamar and herself baptized (LL, 162ff.). Before her baptism she spoke with admiration of Elizabeth Gurley Flynn and other activist women such as those who led the labor strikes in the coal mines. With her entry into the church she developed an admiration and appreciation for Thérèse of Lisieux (about whom she wrote a small book), Teresa of Avila, Catherine of Siena, and other Catholic saints who had lived intense spiritual, religious, moral lives. These, too, receive regular mention in her essays and books. Though she kept in regular contact with friends such as Nina Polcyn (Moore) and Eileen Egan, for example, over many years, and although they were undoubtedly important to her, these friendships never surface as pre-eminent influences in her thinking. Since she did not live with them in community over an extended period of time, it may be that there was little or no opportunity to face conflict and the resolution of conflict with them, as, we shall see later, she did with John Cogley or Jim Forest. A fuller picture of Dorothy Day's friendships, and friendships with women in particular, may await the opening of her private papers and correspondence which are now restricted until twenty-five years after her death. A chapter on Dorothy Day, "The Friend," invites attention from those who regarded her as such. From Dorothy's own words, one receives the message that these women were an important presence in her experience of community and family, but not decisive influences in her thinking, envisioning, or acting.[17]

In *Loaves and Fishes*, Day described the Catholic Worker as "an eight-page monthly tabloid paper" (LF, vii) and a movement wherein people lived in community in voluntary poverty in order to feed the hungry, clothe the naked, visit the imprisoned, counsel the doubtful,

---

17. Friendship among women has received fresh attention by philosophers, theologians, and ethicists in recent times. Mary E. Hunt's *Fierce Tenderness: A Feminist Theology of Friendship* is a particularly informative, engaging, and interesting constructive piece. Other examples include Janice Raymond, *A Passion for Friends* and Carter Heyward, *The Redemption of God*.

nurse the sick, and bury the dead. In 1933, when the movement was launched with the publication of the paper (the houses of hospitality developed later, as a response to hungry, unemployed neighbors), the great depression was in its fourth year, there was no social security program, banks had collapsed on a wide scale, and President Roosevelt was initiating a wide variety of reform programs, though none of these ended the depression nor solved the problems of unemployment. After thirty years, Day published *Loaves and Fishes*, an account of the Catholic Worker, cast in five parts: (1) historical beginnings, (2) the importance and value of voluntary poverty, (3) portraits of selected personalities, (4) a sampling of memorable events, and (5) the central place given to the practice of love.

Essays on Peter Maurin and Ammon Hennacy give personalized portraits of the convictions that informed Catholic Worker efforts— poverty, nonviolence, personal responsibility, the works of mercy. In these essays particularly, Day wrote as reporter, friend, and loving critic. Although Peter brought vision, a knowledge of history, and a lack of self-concern that appealed greatly to Dorothy, he also had annoying habits, like failing to bathe and not knowing when to stop talking. Ammon was to Dorothy something of a prophet, if a boastful one, preaching and practicing nonviolent resistance. Ammon was normally "irritatingly right" and "often hard to take" (LF, 104). His love for attention and flair for the dramatic brought him both critics and admirers. That was fine with Ammon; he "would prefer having people speak of him adversely to their not mentioning him at all. Hatred or love he can accept, but indifference, no" (LF, 104).

As an astute reporter of people, Day also portrayed less well-known figures like Anna, a bag lady and Catholic Worker guest for five years; Maurice O'Connell, a Catholic Worker "terror," "an implacable tyrant" (LF, 53), and the community's "collective trial" (LF, 125); Mr. Breen, an out and out racist (LF, 35–38), and other guests. With fascinating, often humorous, and always distinctive detail she described the inclinations, contributions, virtues, and vices of Catholic Worker editors and cooks, writers and farmers. She wanted her readers, as herself, to have a realistic understanding of love as hard work. Not allowing her readers to romanticize community life, she portrayed community members with all their warts. Reflecting on these anecdotal and biographical sketches, Day voiced her uncertainty about how best to understand and depict people. Because she sought realism in these passages, she was quite willing to acknowledge the distress, strain, and difficulty of loving those who were in some respects notably unlovable. One of her purposes was to comfort her readers, knowing that "many in this world have old or sick or sinful people with whom they have to live, whom they have to love" (LF, 54).[18]

One of her arrests and imprisonments (for refusing to cooperate with air raid drills) was used as a lens into prison life where the reader meets Matilda, Baby Doll, and numerous unnamed prisoners whose miseries and outrage are empathetically reported. Dorothy's brief but memorable encounters with famous Catholic Worker visitors like Joseph and John Kennedy, Evelyn Waugh, and W. H. Auden punctuate this story about otherwise quite ordinary folk who gravitated to the Catholic Worker for a great variety of motivations. Workers came to live their ideals, to find themselves, to seek excitement and adventure, to leave the monotony of their jobs (LF, 131). Neighborhood guests came to eat, to wait, to find someone to talk to in order to lighten their troubles (LF, 205). Sometimes the distinction between Worker and guest dissolved when guests stayed on and became Workers. Day believed that she was her brother and sister's keeper (LF, 88). Each exchange reminded her anew "how much ordinary kindness can do" (LF, 172).

> It never ceased to grieve me how quickly men could lose their dignity when they were down-and-out. . . . For this reason, we never asked any questions of these wounded ones. . . . We only tried . . . to make them feel at home, and . . . to help them in regaining some measure of self-respect. [LF, 60–61]

> We never ask people why they are here. They just come from the streets to eat, to wait, to find some place for themselves, to have someone to talk to, someone with whom to share and so to lighten their troubles. [LF, 205]

Day's assessment of their work was both sympathetic and critical. She judged that she and Peter and others had cast their net too broadly by trying to be all things to all people: they had tried to run an agronomic university, a retreat house, an old people's home, a shelter for delinquent boys and expectant mothers, a graduate school for the study of communities, religions, the state, war and peace. Recognizing they had aimed high, Day hoped they had achieved enough at least "to arouse the conscience," as Peter had hoped (LF, 200). When she compared this work with other projects, such as the *kibbutzim* in Israel,

---

18. A June 1977 entry ("On Pilgrimage," *The Catholic Worker*, 2) notes that out of fifty people who then inhabited the Third Street Catholic Worker house, (only) nine were "utterly reliable, intelligent and trained."

the reclaiming of the desert, the reforestation of bare hillsides, she found her work and Peter's feeble by comparison: "How little we have attempted, let alone accomplished" (LF, 204). Yet hope persisted: that by their effort, their struggle, their sufferings and failures, they had been able to "unleash forces that help to overcome the evil in the world" (LF, 204).

When autobiography is viewed as a creative, constructive, and interpretive enterprise as well as a project of remembering, recollecting, and recording, the autobiographer is viewed as both creator and creation. Day's autobiographical writings are both process and product in which memory and meaning were brought to bear on a series of experiences that are emphasized, juxtaposed, commented upon, or omitted. In autobiography, the author tells *a* story rather than *the* story and tells it *this* way rather than *that* way. The autobiographer selects, interprets, and orders memory, meaning, and message in the form of memoir, apology, confession, and autobiographical novel. "She may even create several, sometimes competing stories about or versions of herself."[19] Day's stories are basically two.

When presenting herself in the persona of June in *The Eleventh Virgin*, Dorothy portrayed a self who thrashed about in prolonged adolescence, searching— sometimes deliberatively, sometimes desperately—for a sense of what to do and what to stand for, seeking a cause and a credo, work, friendship, love, and intimacy. The search remained unresolved at novel's end, as it had remained unresolved in Dorothy's life at that time. The self-portrayals in *Union Square*, *Long Loneliness*, and *Loaves and Fishes*, by contrast, reveal a much more finely focused sense of self due to the central role religious and community commitments came to play in Dorothy's life and due to the resolution of her own identity questions concerning love, intimacy, meaningful work, religion, and God. Once she moved beyond adolescence into adult self-definition, four images emerged with force. Day perceived and presented herself as *writer*, *woman*, *religious*, and *radical*.

As *writer*, Day displayed an acute sensitivity to what was going on around her (just as her father had taught her) and a skill for communicating her observations simply and clearly (LF, 7). She admirably combined the reporter's instinct to notice, observe, inquire, and record, together with the editor's drive to make judgments and voice opinions. Her descriptions about what went on in the slums of New York City as well as the eccentricities of what occurred in Catholic Worker houses and farms are clear and clean samples of straightforward prose. At the

---

19. Sidonie Smith, *A Poetics of Women's Autobiography*, 46–47, also 45.

same time, her concerns and values were equally straightforward; the reader senses Day's discontent through narratives of sadness, misery, tragedy, bad luck, and abuse that accompany being poor. Her descriptions of joyous occasions are equally vivid and always about common human pleasures, such as affection and delight between friends, the beauty of a blossoming tree, a simple and succulent feast of mushrooms, eggs, cheese, and coffee.

Writing was important to Dorothy Day the child who kept a notebook in order better to cope with her moments of great happiness and to diffuse her pain (US, 110; LL, 132). Writing became a source of employment in youth and means of appeal to contributors who supported her works of mercy (LF, 86). Writing offered Day time for privacy and reflection in the midst of a demanding, noisy life and a vehicle for arguing her social criticism and pacifist convictions to a broad public audience. As important as writing was to Dorothy Day, however, and as deep a part of her identity as it became, writing became difficult ("harrowingly painful," she put it [LL, 9]) when she knew that people needed her.

Her responsiveness to people in need of care has led one author to call Day *earth mother*.[20] Certainly her sense of herself as *woman and mother* pervades the pages of her books. She regarded herself as the mother, later the grandmother, of a large, "far-flung family" (LF, 138), and willingly assumed the tasks of loving, comforting (LF, 54), and feeding others (LF, 83, 86, 89, 211; cf. OP, 34). She valued the power of simple, faithful presence and mused in one journal entry that she wished one of her forthcoming grandchildren would be named Fidel or Constance, for fidelity and constancy were her favorite virtues.

Dorothy's long view of her life was that she had always had religious interests and inclinations (US, 159; LL, 10), and that although she had resisted these (US, 39, 42, 88, 132, 138–39, 143; LL, 40, 46, 96), her spiritual inclinations ultimately accounted for her conversion. She recognized herself, in a word, as a *religious person*, attuned to the reality and presence of God.

Throughout her adulthood, Day saw herself as a *radical*. Once she fell "in love with the masses" (US, 48) through her direct observations and with the help of some favorite authors, she found ways to be with the workers and the poor by working and living in their neighborhoods, writing and marching on their behalf (LL, 43, 58, 124), and praying with them in city churches (US, 15, 89).

With respect to current discussion that women's autobiographies

---

20. Debra Campbell, "The Catholic Earth Mother."

emphasize the personal over the historical and family life over career, and utilize a disjunctiveness in literary form rather than a progressive and tightly unified narrative form, Day's work requires more nuancing than these categories contain. The personal/historical, private/public dimensions of Day's life are both represented in her writings; her observations and thoughts move readily and easily from one to the other. As a radical who lived at the margins of conventional social mores, Day's personal story is embedded in the events of history (the labor movement, the Russian Revolution, the I.W.W. activities, the numerous wars that mark this century), and history is made intensely personal in the record of her feelings, convictions, ambivalences, and hopes. As this chapter suggests and as the following chapters demonstrate in further detail, Day did not belabor any opposition or dichotomy between "public" and "private," "historical" and "personal," nor did she struggle to combine or integrate two aspects of life which were somehow preconceived or experienced as opposed or conflictual. As a communitarian radical by inclination and choice, Day operated out of a fundamental sense of connection between the public and the private.[21] As one attuned to the downside of industrialization and urbanization on masses of people who became excluded from active societal participation, Day urged the development of agricultural and craftsmanlike skills to encourage individual productivity and participation. The privatization of the family and the split between home and work that came with industrialization were not congenial to Dorothy Day's radical, communitarian sensibilities. The personal events, feelings, and choices she lived through and lived out were fed by the facts of history. Conversely, historical events and movements regularly motivated and mobilized her moral affections, judgments, and actions.

Day took her work as a given. She would be uneasy with the word *career*. Its connotations of self-concern, professional development, reputation, and success would be alien to her social sensibilities and moral idealism. Day had work to do, not a career to be carved. As one whose sense of self was shaped by the powerful experience of pregnancy and childbirth, Day became exceedingly conscious of herself as woman and mother, yet she never seemed to cast the mother in her and the worker in her in any opposition. She took it as a given that she had a distinctive voice to speak to questions of public and social policy precisely because of her being a woman and mother. As will be noted in later chapters, one of her arguments decrying war and war-based economies

21. For an important discussion of these themes, see Eli Zaretsky, *Capitalism, the Family, and Personal Life*. Also Rosemary Ruether's excellent essay on "Home and Work: Women's Roles and the Transformation of Values."

was grounded in the fact that war destroyed and separated families. The work of resisting conscription, air raid drills, preparations for war, and war itself was "woman's work" for Dorothy Day just as much as washing and cooking and tending babies. As a radical by orientation, a single parent by circumstance and choice, and a writer by inclination and need for income, she took it as a given that work outside the home was not only a fact of life, but, more to the point, an opportunity to effect needed social change.

From Union Square to Rome, *The Long Loneliness*, and *Loaves and Fishes* each contain a medley of forms, as noted above: personal narrative, journal entry, religious essay, meditation, biographical sketch, anecdote, self-critical analysis. Only the novel, *The Eleventh Virgin*, sustains a single (narrative) form. Day's sense of self as "a journalist and a diarist pure and simple" (rather than as a writer of books [LL, 183]) provides some explanation for the multiplicity and therefore disjunctiveness of form that we find in her publications. Her editor and colleague Stanley Vishnewski explained that most of her writing was accomplished on the run, in fragments (M, 4). Day herself admitted how "harrowingly painful" it was to take time out for writing when she knew that people needed her (LL, 9). Wanting to impress upon readers the importance she placed on the practice of the works of mercy, on personal direct action in response to human need, she wrote: "Peter and I feel that the work is more important than the talking and the writing about the work" (M, 24).

Yet in spite of these explanations and disclaimers, writing was the central work of this autobiographer-reporter-novelist-diarist-journalist-editor-publisher. Writing to inform and to persuade was serious business for Day who sustained this commitment over a period of sixty-five years. Writing was one of her dearly valued "works of mercy." The works of mercy—which meant feeding the hungry, giving drink to the thirsty, clothing the naked, sheltering the homeless, visiting the sick, burying the dead, informing the ignorant, persuading the doubtful, protesting and resisting evil, comforting the victims of evil, challenging (and also forgiving) the doers of evil, and praying for the living and the dead—included writing. For even though she insisted that writing *about* the work was less important than *doing* the work, her fundamental position was that writing (to inform, persuade, and encourage action) was an act fraught with moral importance, one of the works of mercy.

We write in response to what we care about, what we believe to be important, what we want to share with others. I have never stopped wanting to do so. I have been reached so many times by certain writers. What is this distinction between writing and doing that some people make? Each is an act. Both can be part of a person's *response*, an ethical response to the world.[22]

---

22. Quoted in Robert Coles, *A Spectacle Unto the World: The Catholic Worker Movement*, xi-xii.

2

THE WOMAN:
ALLY AND CRITIC OF
FEMINISM

D AY'S SENSE OF SELF AS WOMAN AND MOTHER, and later, grandmother, pervades her writings. Given recent interest in women's issues,
concerns, and social expectations, a number of questions regarding
Dorothy Day's views about women and the choices she self-consciously
made as a woman invite attention. For example, did Day's views about
women conform to and reflect the conventional patriarchal outlook of
her mentor Peter Maurin, whose theology identified man with spirit and
woman with matter? (OPS, 362) Or was Dorothy Day a "feminist"[1] as
at least one scholar has claimed? If so, in what sense was Day a
feminist? If not, what indeed were her views about women and women's
roles? How did she describe women, reflect on them, and present them
to her readers?

Since Day grew up during the early twentieth-century suffrage
movement, joined her first march in Washington, D.C., on its behalf in
1917 and received a sentence of thirty days in jail for her actions (she
was released after sixteen days when President Wilson signed a pardon
for the whole group), one might think that Day supported the cause of
suffrage and identified with the movement advocating voting rights and
other equities for women. But her account of this event tells us some-

---

1. Patricia F. McNeal, *The American Catholic Peace Movement 1928–1972*, 37.

thing altogether different. "The cause for which we were in jail seemed utterly unimportant," she wrote. "I had not much interest in the vote, and it seemed to me our protest should have been not for ourselves but for all those thousands of prisoners throughout the country, victims of a materialistic system" (US, 86). Day's dissatisfaction with the suffrage movement can be understood as one feature of her anarchist sympathies and as one aspect of her critique of American socioeconomic values. She viewed the movement as a narrow middle-class effort to effect change in one limited area, when, in her estimation, many areas required radical change.

As a person attracted to anarchism, Day never used the vote women won (OPS, 304). She distrusted government, valuing personal responsibility in the context of caring community far more highly than state structures. "The vote," she thought, simply provided for women an opportunity to participate in a way of life that had a skewed sense of values: materialism, violence, and social patterns that promoted injustice and indifference toward the working poor, the unemployed, and the homeless. Day could not envision what good women's suffrage would do when it came, for she found those women who would most likely use the vote to be blindly patriotic and supportive of the American system.[2] The suffragists themselves boasted that they brought forth a great middle-of-the-road movement that was neither radical nor reactionary. Dorothy Day's radical perspective and proclivities were insufficiently addressed for her to become engaged by this approach. Historian Aileen Kraditor describes the movement as "an association primarily of white, native-born, middle-class American women between 1890 and 1920" who equated political liberation with Anglo-Saxon ancestry. Although Dorothy Day shared their ancestry, the women's "anti-Negro, antiforeign, frequently antilabor attitudes" together with "their defense of American democracy and the principles of the Declaration of Independence"[3] would have distanced Day from the start. Her fundamental experience while in jail with the suffrage marchers was one of solitude, not solidarity (US, 86).

Day was offended by Emma Goldman's advocacy of free love and of the tendency of women revolutionaries to complicate social analysis

---

2. Gerda Lerner's judgment in 1971 corroborates Day's reservations about women's suffrage. In *The Woman in American History*, 172, Lerner writes that the winning of suffrage proved a disappointment, for although women voted, they did not vote in recognizable blocs nor did they use their votes to improve society; also they failed to win political power so that although they were a majority of the population they remained a negligible minority in political representation.

3. Kraditor, "Woman Suffrage in Perspective," 220–22.

and social change by emphasizing personal needs. She universalized that "men are the single-minded, the pure of heart, in these movements. Women by their very nature are more materialistic, thinking of the home, the children, and of all things needful to them, especially love" (LL, 68–69). In constantly searching to meet these needs, she felt, women went against their own best interests (LL, 69). In the voice of June in *The Eleventh Virgin*, Day noted the limitations of the suffragist vision by highlighting the conflicting concerns of the participants and their failure to work together; some fought for the vote, others for birth control, still others for street women or for pacifism, and often one group criticized the other:[4] "if I worked among these people with their single-track minds, I'd go crazy . . . . I feel that all these people with their causes are one-sided" (EV, 217). What was needed, she felt, "was a radical party whose platform would include such planks as birth control, pacifism, suffrage" all in one (EV, 209).

Day's interest in the dignity and respect due the worker and her later support for the labor movement did move her to appreciate the leadership of those women who led labor strikes in order to shorten the working day (from twelve and fifteen hours), increase wages, and support worker organization and participation in policy decisions: "My heart thrilled at those unknown women in New England who led the first strikes to liberate the women and children from the cotton mills" (US, 49; see also LL, 51). She found Elizabeth Gurley Flynn's "fire and vision" particularly "thrilling" and memorable (LL, 60–61, 75).[5] Her admiration for the working class, who were never more than a small minority among suffragists,[6] led her to prefer revolutionary, not merely reformist visions of change.

Having attributed her religious faith to her personal experiences as lover, wife, and mother, Day felt that it was precisely in the direct and

---

4. In *Anarchist Women 1870–1920*, 47, Margaret Marsh offers a supporting judgment: "Feminism was not a set of specific beliefs and demands, despite the tendency of a later generation of scholars to subsume the whole movement into the drive for suffrage; it was a vast, complicated, and often contradictory movement."
    5. Elizabeth Gurley Flynn (1890–1964), an I.W.W. activist and later Communist, tells the story of her early life in *The Rebel Girl: An Autobiography (My First Life 1906–1926)*; other relevant works on her views and experiences are *The Alderson Story* and Rosalyn Fraad Baxandall, ed., *Words on Fire: The Life and Writings of Elizabeth Gurley Flynn*. In *Love Is the Measure*, 211, James Forest notes that when Flynn died (in the Soviet Union), her small estate of clothes, books, and furniture went to the Catholic Worker.
    Although Day does not mention labor and strike leader Mother Jones (Mary Harris Jones [1830–1930]) by name, Jim Forest writes that Day was familiar with her as well as with Elizabeth Gurley Flynn (*Love Is the Measure*, 19). See *Autobiography of Mother Jones* and *Mother Jones Speaks*.
    6. Kraditor, "Woman Suffrage in Perspective," 225.

creative actions of sexuality, love, pregnancy, and childbirth that she was drawn to acknowledge the creative source of all.

> I had known Forster a long time before we contracted our common-law relationship, and I have always felt that it was life with him that brought me natural happiness, that brought me to God. His ardent love of creation brought me to the Creator of all things . . . .
> I could not see that love between a man and woman was incompatible with love of God. God is the Creator, and the very fact that we were begetting a child made me have a sense that we were made in the image and likeness of God, co-creators with him. [LL, 153]

In spite of the fact that she had been willing to bear her child outside of a legally sanctioned marriage and remained an anarchist as a Catholic, Day's occasional references to marriage reflect conventional views. When describing a marital decision to become involved in social action, for example, she wrote that "as head of the household" the husband did not need to consider the wife when making social action commitments, though the wife "of course" (OP, 159) must consider her husband when making such decisions. Day often accepted traditional, conventional roles assigned to men and women, which she found operative and confirmed in her experience.

> Women do love to be active, it is natural to them, they are most happy in doing that for which they are made, when they are cooking and serving others. They are the nourishers, starting with the babies at the breast and from there on their work is to nourish and strengthen and console. [OP, 40; see also 174, 34]

Struggling to interpret Peter Maurin's statement that "woman is matter, man is spirit," Day came to interpret this to mean that woman was most completely herself when "caring for the growing things, providing for them, feeding them, clothing them. It is not an empty phrase—'Mother Earth,' fecund, warm, rich, constant and silent."[7]

Day's journals provide vivid detail of women's work. When describing the life of a mother on a farm, for example, she displayed the never-ending bending and lifting which mark the woman's day: "cook-

---

7. Dorothy Day, "Peter and Women," 189.

ing, dishwashing, clothes washing, drawing water, keeping two fires going, feeding babies, consoling babies, picking up after babies" (OP, 7). This back-breaking work, however, later led her to critical musings about hardened gender roles: "One cannot help thinking that the men have an easier time of it. It is wonderful to work out on such a day as this with the snow falling lightly all around, chopping wood, dragging in fodder, working with the animals. Women are held pretty constantly to the house" (OP, 27; see also M, 36, 43–44).

Day registered a more pronounced measure of discontent regarding gender roles when she accounted for the first issue of *The Catholic Worker*. Explaining her decision as editor not to give the lead editorial to Peter Maurin and his three-point program, she speculated about her reasons for this decision: "Perhaps it sounded too utopian for my tastes; perhaps I was irked because women were left out in his description of a house of hospitality, where he spoke of a group of men living under a priest" (LF, 22).[8] A skillful journalist, Day served as reporter of events and ideas, often offering response and commentary but generally avoiding extensive, discursive analysis. This may have been due to a feeling of ambivalence about her intellectual skills. On the one hand, she exhibited self-confidence when she registered annoyance at the way "men, even priests" insulted women's intelligence with "pious pap" (BL,189). And yet, on the other hand, she seems to have internalized the insult, for she often attributed to her identity as a woman a certain "stupidity" (HH, xxxvi), a "wandering mind" (HH, 2), and an inability to understand theological subtleties (US, 169).[9]

Such examples suggest that not only was Day not an advocate of women's suffrage, she was not a feminist in any self-conscious, intentional, or public way. She spurned sociopolitical feminism, refusing to march on behalf of women's rights; she was no closet feminist either, since she regularly critiqued the movement in both its early and later twentieth-century forms as being too self-centered.[10]

She did observe inequities in socially assigned gender roles and expectations and occasionally voiced these as journalistic observations and personal musings. At times she represented and reflected the patriarchal attitude toward women whose difference from men is interpreted as a kind of inferiority. This accepted inferiority then functioned

8. Maurin's program of action (round-table discussions, houses of hospitality, and agronomic universities or farming communes) appeared in the second issue of *The Catholic Worker* (June–July 1933). A more extensive presentation, where he spoke of the role of priests and bishops, appeared in the October 1933 issue.
9. Coles, *Radical Devotion*, 117.
10. Patricia McGowan, "Somebody Loves You When You're Down and Out," 30.

on her behalf as a way of explaining to her readers her limitations as
author. As a woman, she wrote, she did not display theological sophis-
tication (US, 169); because she was a woman, she explained to her
reader, ordinary "daily doings" (HH, 2) pervaded her writings.
Dorothy Day's writings yield numerous observations that conform
to a conventional patriarchal outlook wherein women were accepted as
naturally and instinctively different from men. This assumed difference
was regularly identified with inferiority or often enough implied it. Yet I
find a hidden feminist dimension to Day's thought, for her work is also
punctuated with observations and recommendations that clearly reflect
a critical eye with respect to injustice in sex roles and a desire to expand
and improve opportunities for women and men alike. The "women's
movement" was not a cause Day committed herself to. She became a
voice on behalf of laborers, pacifists, and nonviolent protestors for
social change, the majority of whom were men. But along the way Day
did voice some critical complaints about inequities between the sexes,
illustrating affinities with the feminist critique, and she placed theological as well as social and personal value on the fact that a greater balance
or integration of gender roles was possible and desirable. As an activist,
Day had believed stoutly in the importance of putting ideas into direct
action and of using actions to arouse the conscience and to stimulate
thought. Her words, by her own standards, then, need to be interpreted
in light of the choices, actions, and commitments that comprised her
life. Doing so provides reason to claim that Day was not only a critic of
feminism but also an ally.

Although she remembered her father as a stern and distant man
who believed that the place for women and children was in the home,
Dorothy the young adult apparently felt otherwise, for she began living
and working independently after spending two years at the University
of Illinois (1914–16) as a student. Her father's discomfort and impa-
tience with her radical ideas moved him, she felt, to treat her in her
adult years as a casual friend, thus sustaining the sense of distance she
had always felt from him as a child. Nonetheless, she pursued her
interests in observing and writing about people who knew poverty,
hunger, and destitution.

Living and working among radical writers (Floyd Dell and Max
Eastman, editors of the leftist monthly *Masses*, Mike Gold, assistant
editor of the socialist *Call*, and reporter John Reed), Dorothy pursued
direct experience with dissenters, anarchists, and labor organizers
(such as the I.W.W.) who often poised themselves in conflict with the
law. Strikes, acts of civil disobedience and other forms of protest
brought with them risk of arrest, abuse, and imprisonment. Imprison-

ment in Chicago in 1922 left her feeling victimized. In contrast to her imprisonment in Washington, D.C., five years earlier with feminist marchers, Day recalled the Chicago episode as one of injustice: "Now I was to have a solitary taste of the injustice, or the ugliness of men's justice, which set me more squarely on the side of the revolution" (LL, 114). Specifically this meant the humiliating experiences of the arrest: being "forced to dress . . . in the presence of two detectives, leering"; being wrongly booked as an inmate of a disorderly house; being forced to stand on the street under the gaze of passers-by while awaiting the police wagon; being put in a room that smelled foul and had an un-screened toilet; being examined for venereal diseases; being unfree to contact lawyer or friend; being judged guilty before trial; being stripped naked and searched for drugs (LL, 115–21). (Eventually Dorothy was released and the case dismissed.)

Reflecting on the Chicago arrest years later, recording it from some distance and in light of her faith and religious sensibilities, Day broadened her view, faulting her own naiveté and her stubbornness in flaunting convention, as well as the Red hysteria at the time (LL, 116). But it is interesting to note that the humiliating injustices she felt only "set [her] more squarely on the side of the revolution" (LL, 114).

In *Loaves and Fishes*, Day reported the feeling of women prostitutes who felt the injustice of being arrested while the men went free (168); she also noted contrasting prison conditions for men and women.

Shut in by walls, bars, concrete, and heavy iron screenings so that even from the roof one's vision of the sky is impeded, mind and body suffer from the strain. Nerves clamor for change, for open air, more freedom of movement.

By contrast,

The men imprisoned over on Hart Island and Riker's Island can get out and play ball, can work on the farm or in the tree nursery. They can see all around them—water and boats and seagulls—and breathe the sea air coming from the Atlantic. [LF, 169]

The revolution Day wanted in those early years, well before her religious conversion and baptism in 1927, is notably of a piece with the revolution she sought to create through the Catholic Worker from 1933 on. As newspaper writers and frequent lecturers, Maurin and Day both saw themselves at work at a task that sought to create the news, not merely to report it. The news they wished to create was a more just society wherein the social teachings of the Catholic encyclicals (*The Condition of Labor* [1891], *The Reconstruction of the Social Order* [1931], would be brought alive and made practical to the lives of workers and the unemployed in the United States.[11]

Feeding the hungry became the primary vehicle for reaching people in need. "A man has to eat," Day said, in characteristic matter-of-fact definitiveness (OPS, 81). There may be murderers among them in their soup kitchen, she admitted, but no matter, no questions, a man has to eat. Feeding the hungry, however, was not sufficient. There had to be learning, discussion of the ideas that would foster a new society in which it would be easier for people to be good. Thus it was through a variety of media, round-table discussions over meals, promulgation of their views in newspaper format, explanatory lectures, and letters of appeal, that Day and Maurin sought to carry on their revolution. Stimulated by the values of empathy for others, personal responsibility in meeting the needs of others, political actions which resisted the materialism, consumerism, and violence of American society, theirs was a revolution designed to alert people to a sense of interdependence and solidarity so that together they might expand a system that favored the wealthy, the powerful, and the bright to include the poor, the weak, and the diminished.

A prominent theme in current feminist ethics is recognition of the connections among a wide range of social injustices: discrimination on the basis of gender, color, culture, age, sexuality, and, some would add, species.[12] Day shared this point of view; she remarked, for example, that the place of sex was as pertinent to questions of social justice as were discussions of war, overpopulation, capital punishment, birth control, abortion, euthanasia, and the role of the state. She saw all of these issues as issues of power and control: "The entire question of man's control over the life of others, over the life forces within man, is one of the most profound importance today" (OPS, 90). In the early years of the Catholic Worker movement, Day focused attention on the labor movement, the evils of war, and the poverty of destitution. In the course of time, she continued to identify and support newly emerging causes of justice: the Cuban revolution, the civil rights quests of the black community in the United States, the work on behalf of better conditions for migrant workers in California and elsewhere, the resistance to U.S.

---

11. Later encyclicals and conciliar documents about social conditions which Day would cite include *Christianity and Social Progress* (1961), *Peace on Earth* (1963), and *The Church in the Modern World* (1965).

12. Beverly Harrison, *Making the Connections*; Rosemary Ruether, *Sexism and God-Talk*; Sallie McFague, *Models of God*.

involvement in Vietnam. She spoke and wrote admiringly and with empathy for Fidel Castro, Martin Luther King, Jr., and Cesar Chavez (OPS, 300[13]); and she encouraged young men to refuse being drafted into the war in Indochina. Notably absent in this list of issues that won Day's attention and public support is the women's movement of the 1960s and 1970s. This can be accounted for in several ways.

To the extent that "the women's movement" was voiced initially and primarily by educated, middle-class white women, arguing for legal, economic, and political reforms, its call for change was insufficiently radical to converge with Day's criticisms of American life and empathy for the underclass. Middle-class women were indeed excluded from power and position in American life, but "middle class" meant "privilege" from the standpoint of the poor, the homeless, the unemployed and unemployable. The critique of the educated urban and suburban feminists did not penetrate the experience of women in the slum, ghetto, and bowery, where Day lived and thought, felt and worked.

Women's liberation is very necessary because women have always been minimized and underpaid; but a great deal of it is too self-centered. It's not geared to the poor, but to articulate middle-class women with time on their hands, the ones who have the least to complain about. Among the poor the position of women is dreadful.[14]

To the extent that the publicized and televised voices of feminism placed a decided emphasis on freedom as a means of securing a broad range of rights for women and arguing for full participation by women in social, political, economic, educational, commercial, and religious structures, they and Day differed in emphases. Dorothy Day's approach to "increasing" the "amount" of justice in the world was not one of accenting freedom but of accenting responsibility. Although she certainly believed in freedom and was jailed on behalf of it, she did not speak in terms of freedom. Rather, she acted out of a personal freedom and urged others to do the same while highlighting always that the important point was how one used one's freedom, namely, for the neighbor, through the works of mercy.

---

13. "We are certainly not Marxist socialists, nor do we believe in violent revolution. Yet we do believe it is better to revolt, to fight, as Castro did with his handful of men, than to do nothing" (OPS, 301–2).

14. Patricia McGowan, "Somebody Loves You When You're Down and Out," 30.

This insistence on responsibility illustrates the focus Day placed on the communitarian features of human existence and on the obligations to one another that arise from the social nature of human persons. Community consistently received the accent in her reading of the interdependent relationship between individual and community. She assumed the importance and power of the individual and placed her emphasis on the good the individual could effect for the group. Attention was not placed on individual rights, but rather on the individual's responsibilities, less on "me," more on "we." Ideally, the worker would strike in order to draw attention to the workers' unfair and unsafe conditions; the unemployed would demonstrate in order to draw attention to the dehumanizing impact of nonparticipation in the economic order.

Insofar as the women's movement emphasized rights over responsibilities and focused on freedom rather than justice, it failed to engage Dorothy Day. She was never drawn to petition or demand equality for women; rather, she was driven to expose and to criticize the system that prevented it in specific forums such as the labor movement, the prison system, and the war resistance movements. "Equality," indeed, was not one of her words. "Participation" better captures her ideal. As a humanistic anarchist by inclination and a Catholic by choice, she affirmed the dignity and respect due to human persons regardless of gender, class, employment status, religion, or race. Her concern was with their participation, particularly economic participation in the face of social marginalization and exclusion.[15] She viewed "distributism" and the "cooperative ideal" as hopeful models of social arrangements that could more adequately foster the common good (HH, 142–49; OPS, 105–7).

Why Dorothy Day did not identify with the pacifist feature of the women's rights movements in the early decades of this century may simply be a factor of her age. Almost all of the women's rights organizations of the late nineteenth and twentieth centuries envisioned peace as

---

15. In *Holding Their Own: American Women in the 1930s*, 136, Susan Ware wonders why women on the left in the 1930s were not "fueled by feminist consciousness" in the way their counterparts were in the 1960s. She offers three explanations: (1) that their participation in the radical movements of the 1930s might have allowed them more scope than the New Left allowed in the 1960s; (2) "that they were unwilling or unable to generalize from their own experiences to a full-scale critique of women's roles in society"; and (3) that their commitment to revolutionary socialism with an emphasis on economic solutions to address social problems subsumed their hopes for a feminist vision (which they read, rightly or wrongly, as selfish, personal, and divorced from economic issues).

part of their vision for a new society.[16] Yet these very movements suffered a decline in visibility, membership, and impact after 1920, just the time when Dorothy Day was coming into her own as a self-defining adult.

To the extent that the "sexual liberation" of women was a component of women's liberation in the 1960s and 1970s, Day would have been bothered, indeed, disapproving, as she had been earlier in the century. She knew from experience what a sexuality liberated from marital commitment could be like. In *The Eleventh Virgin* she had recorded and explored the experiences of sexual awakening, seduction, and surrender, and with these the experiences of humiliation, insult, and abandonment. In *The Long Loneliness* she alluded to a similar set of experiences which she publicly repudiated. Her dislike of Emma Goldman's ethic of free love sustained itself throughout Day's life. Indeed, her views on sexuality became solidified and supported by her religious commitments and the theology of her chosen church.

Day regarded sex as an appealing, beautiful, powerful, and profound life force, which, when rightly engaged in, met many human needs and desires. Sexual love could satisfy, console, nourish, comfort, and heal. Sex could also create life and thus was to be seen as a creative force expressing the creative love and work of God.[17] For Day, sex was fundamentally related to the integrity and life of the family, which she regarded as the context for children's growth and understanding of stability and commitment (OPS, 159). To the extent that the "women's liberation movement" connoted a sexual liberation which separated sexual activity from marital commitment and from the possibility of (procreative) "co-creation," it failed to win Day's interest and support.[18]

---

16. Rosemary Ruether, "Women and Peace," in Andolsen et al., eds., *Women's Consciousness, Women's Conscience*, 63–74. See also Berenice Carroll, "Feminism and Pacifism: Historical and Theoretical Connections," and Marie Louise Degen, *The History of the Woman's Peace Party* (the Woman's Peace Party emerged in 1915 and in 1919 became the Women's International League for Peace and Freedom). Current accounts of women's peace collectives and women's peace actions can be found in the Cambridge Women's Peace Collective, *My Country Is the Whole World: An Anthology of Women's Work on Peace and War*, and the 1988 special edition of *Women's Studies International Forum*, ed. Berenice A. Carroll and Jane E. Mohraz, a report on nonviolent direct action women's groups around the world.

17. William Miller, *All Is Grace*, 164–68.

18. For a vivid contrast that explains Day's comments about Emma Goldman, see Goldman's essay, "Marriage and Love," in *Anarchism and Other Essays*, 233–45.

In two separate 1975 entries, Day briefly addressed the issue of lesbianism, one in an understanding tone, the other a disapproving tone. She felt that women needed companionship with other women in the face of their frequent loneliness and that this need was often at the root of lesbianism (see Patricia McGowan, "Somebody Loves You When

During the 1970s, the final decade of her life, Day wrote and published less often, due to failing health.[19] It was at this time that the feminist critique deepened and broadened. Self-critical debates within feminism expanded it beyond its white middle-class origins to include the specific concerns of women of color. And the political focus of feminism expanded to include historical, philosophical, and theological analysis of sexism, androcentrism, patriarchy, and misogyny. Feminism began to address fundamental issues about how knowledge is constructed and disseminated, and by whom. Just as the movement was gaining energy and strength, Dorothy Day was losing energy and strength. Feminism and Day thus failed to meet as public allies.

Without underestimating the conflicts between them, it is nonetheless useful to note several areas of compatibility and convergence of view between stated feminist concerns and Dorothy Day's views and choices. One point of consonance, noted above, was the sense of connection among diverse social problems (sex, race, war, capital punishment, abortion, and the like) and a desire to address these problems from a fundamental and integral vision of justice.

Another pertains to the feminist affirmation of the legitimacy, need, and wisdom of women's participation in the work force. Dorothy Day was herself a model of full and active participation. Although she did not work for a salary at the Catholic Worker, but lived frugally from contributions in order to distribute funds to the poor and to voice their needs in lectures and articles, she worked. Conscious always of the need to pay the bills (rent, grocer, post office, and printer), she wrote in order to secure income as well as to make known her views on life. She edited a newspaper, lectured widely, fed the hungry, clothed the poor, found housing for the homeless, purchased farms for the cultivation of the land and employment of the unemployed. She publicly protested the advocacy and acceptance of war through marches, pickets, sit-ins, and vigils of support. She herself lived the life of working woman and working mother, meeting the demands of multiple commitments, though in an admittedly unconventional way.

In 1965, reflecting on her daughter Tamar's opportunity to train as a nurse, Day voiced approving thoughts about women working outside

You're Down and Out," 30). In a letter to Sister Peter Claver (8 September 1975), Day makes clear her disapproval (quoted in Mary Purpura, "Dorothy Day," 124 and 136).

19. In the March 1975 issue of *The Catholic Worker*, Dorothy announced her retirement from day-to-day responsibilities, yet continued her writing, often about experiences of her past. In the January 1977 issue she defended this focus in response to those who described her columns as "reminiscences," by insisting on the importance, indeed the "obligation," to keep the memories of people's experiences alive. Her last column of "On Pilgrimage" appeared in the October 1980 issue. She died 29 November 1980.

the home. She encouraged her daughter's decision to attend nursing school by pledging to care for Tamar's children during the four months training time Tamar would be away. Day explained her thinking:

> With children all day in school women have come to feel the isolation of the home, the lack of community facilities such as day nurseries. They know they have a contribution to make to the common good. Their talents are unused and undeveloped. And above all, there is the crucial need to earn money to help support and to educate and provide training in turn for the young ones. [OPS, 202]

Day thus recognized the multiple motivations that move women to work in the public sphere: economic necessity, the need to overcome the isolation of the nuclear family context, and the desire to make a contribution to the larger community in addition to one's immediate family.[20]

Day would not, I propose, be sympathetic to the feminist slogan of "having it all." Such a position would alienate Dorothy Day who spent her life praising simplicity and detachment, fidelity and constancy, life lived "by little and by little." Yet Day would, I think, be quite sympathetic to women who want to "do it all" (as distinct from "have it all"). By this I refer to the desire for multiple and diverse commitments: to contribute to the larger, public sphere, to marry, to mother, simultaneously. The accent here is on attending to the world, contributing to the world, working in the world and on behalf of the world, utilizing one's talents and inclinations for those who might be aided by them. To have it all taps a metaphor of consumption; to do it all suggests action in and with others. The second of these slogans fits with Day's outlook in a way the first could not.[21]

---

20. On women priests, she said, "It's a vocation that doesn't attract me but I wouldn't disapprove of it. If there are women premiers and prime ministers, why not a woman pope?" Patricia McGowan, "Somebody Loves You When You're Down and Out," 30.

21. Marc Ellis, who lived at the New York Catholic Worker for nearly a year, comments on the women workers he knew, in *A Year At the Catholic Worker*, 113:

This life of living and working among the poor and the destitute elicits a certain strength of character that is not easily described. Conceivably, it is difficult to describe because our societal image of women is so different from what women at the Worker have become. Here women do not dress for men, or make men the center of their lives. Attraction is not the basis of life, or even a peripheral concern. It is values and ideas which form the focal point of their life. Their strength of character comes from having plunged into living life rather than having been protected from it, from risking the role they were raised to fill, and striking out into the reality of suffering.

The Catholic Worker mission to feed the hungry, clothe the naked, and instruct the ignorant was a mission that engaged men and women alike, encouraging the sharing of tasks regardless of gender. In this setting, men and women were called upon to purchase food, prepare and serve meals, and perform the cleaning and dishwashing tasks required by meal service. Traditionally "woman's work," such tasks shared across gender lines and gender roles were for Day a source of eschatological hope, rooted in a biblically based theology. At the Catholic Worker,

> men joined in the healing and the nourishing, the building and the spinning and the weaving, the cultivation and the preservation of the good earth. Now there is neither bond nor free, Greek or Hebrew, male or female—we are a little nearer to the heavenly kingdom when men are feeding the hungry. It is real action as well as symbolic action. [OPS, 378]

One of her more sympathetic statements about feminist concerns addressed this issue of partnership in work:

> One of the bitter resentments of women is that there's no real companionship and partnership between the man and the woman. All work should be shared. . . . But for the man to come home, sit around, and expect to be waited on, when the woman has been working too, often with nerve-wracking care of troubled children, it is not fair to the woman. There's too much of that. There's no sharing or companionship. St. Paul says that in the Kingdom of God there is no Jew or Gentile, neither bond nor free, neither male nor female.[22]

This very concrete ethic of women and men caring and working in family and community without regard to socially assigned gender roles is a theme regularly voiced in feminist discourse. For Day, this insistence on mutually engaged-in work was not only advisable from a human point of view, but symbolized the heavenly kingdom promised in the Gospels.

Day's views about women touch a prominent feminist hope: recovery of the integral, intimate connections between the personal and the political, the spiritual and the material, the religious and the social-

---

22. Bob Fitch, "Dorothy Day: Witness to a Radical Faith," 41.

historical features of human experience.[23] Day voiced esteem for women's inclination to see the "whole" (BL, 270), women's ability to keep a "balance" (OPS, 378), and women's tendency to "think with their whole bodies" (BL, 270). Thus, upon hearing Peter Maurin's "obscure Thomistic utterance" that "man is spirit, woman is matter" (OPS, 362–63), Dorothy Day interpreted this in a very interesting way: "Woman is close to the material things of life and accepts them, this integration of soul and body and its interaction" (OPS, 363). Rather than perceive it as a view which relegated woman to inferior status, as was often the case in the history of Christian thought,[24] Day accepted this claim as true, and proceeded to understand it in terms of woman's capacity to integrate conflicting features of human life.

Rosemary Ruether writes that it is nearly impossible for an individual to dissent from a culture unless one is supported by a dissenting community that serves also as an alternative community. For it takes a new consciousness, supported by such communities, to isolate and rethink a dominant idea or body of material and see it as a problem rather than as normative.[25] Since Day did not participate in any dissenting community with respect to gender ideology, it is understandable that her alliances with feminist thought are limited to a specific behavior or practice rather than to any underlying feminist consciousness and concomitant analysis. Day had always felt that "people were the product of their environment" (OPS, 187), a belief that enabled her to accept difference and disagreement. She was no exception.[26]

Dorothy Day's interest in ideas, understanding of ideas, and her testing of ideas were all activated by attending to her experience. In this respect, too, her writings exemplify an important feature of feminist ethics: woman's experience as starting point. Her writings are a record of that experience and the insights released by experience. She learned

---

23. See, for example, Charlene Spretnak, ed., *The Politics of Women's Spirituality: Essays on the Rise of Spiritual Power within the Feminist Movement*, and Daniel Maguire, *The Moral Revolution*, particularly "The Feminization of God and Ethics" (105–21) and "The Feminist Turn in Ethics" (122–29).
24. Caroline Walker Bynum, *Holy Feast, Holy Fast*, 161–68 and chap. 6.
25. See Ruether, "The Question of Feminism," 128; also *Sexism and God-Talk*, 183–92.
26. Neither is this author nor this reader an exception, which is precisely why it is important for us actively to invite insight from other communities, traditions, and cultures, enabling us to see as others see and to notice the relativity of perspective with which we ourselves see. This applies to every perspective however named, whether Christian, Marxist, Buddhist, atheist, feminist, patriarchal, etc. For a provocative discussion of women's experience, as men's experience, as socially constructed, see Sheila Greeve Devaney, "The Limits of the Appeal to Women's Experience," esp. 41–48, in Clarissa Atkinson et al., eds., *Shaping New Vision*.

from others as well as from self, from recognized authorities in positions of knowledge and power and from unrecognized authorities met on the streets of New York city, from people who shared her religious faith and from people who repudiated or ignored her faith, from those who agreed with her anarchist perspective and from others who were uneasy with it or even shocked by it. But in all of her encounters, reflections, and records, Dorothy Day's sense of self as woman and mother (not only of Tamar, but of a large, far-flung family) informed, punctuated, and directed her observations and judgments.[27] She had longed for a child years before she gave birth to Tamar, felt profound gratitude over Tamar's birth and would have loved to have had more children. She often wrote about the joys and the hard work that children bring into a woman's life and regarded her Catholic Worker community as a far-flung family. Day brought this awareness to bear on her social activism as well as her family life. This meant that in order to work while rearing a young child, she had had to rely on others for help. In the early years, her brother John and his wife Tessa helped with child care; later, when Day was living at the Catholic Worker on New York's east side, Tamar attended boarding school on Staten Island, and as a teenager spent some years with Catholic Worker artist Ade Bethune's family in Canada and Rhode Island, where she was taught crafts. In Farmingdale, Long Island, she learned farming skills at an agricultural school. As much as she relished her identity as mother, however, Dorothy Day, "The Mother," remains an untold story that only Tamar can write.

As an autobiographer-reporter-writer about life *as experienced*, Day did not indulge in speculation about the origin of the differences she observed between women and men, did not become engaged by nature/nurture theories nor biological/cultural explanations. She simply noted her experience and recorded it, making it available for whatever insight and usefulness it might have for readers. What contemporary readers note is that with respect to feminist questions of gender identity and gender ideology which have received widespread attention in our time, Day's voice is one of both criticism and support.

---

27. Day's attraction to motherhood is evident also in a fantasy exercise John Cogley records. In response to a group discussion on the question "What would you like to do in eternity?" Dorothy's answer was that she would like to be a wife and mother, charged with the care of an ever-growing family (*A Canterbury Tale*, 20).

At various points in her writing, she expressed the joy she received from being with babies (OP, 111); at other points she acknowledged the great discipline and mortification care of babies required of a woman. In the work of caring for babies, she judged, one gets a glimpse of both heaven and hell (M, 43–44).

3

THE CONVERT:
COMMUNIST, CHRISTIAN,
CATHOLIC

ALTHOUGH DOROTHY DAY AS WRITER and Dorothy Day as woman, wife, and mother are deep and powerful images of self that drive Dorothy Day as worker, they are also partial. An accurate picture of Day's self-understanding and self-presentation requires sustained attention to her sense of self as religious. I am particularly interested in the moral dimension of Day's religious journey; throughout my examination of her conversion account, I wish to be alert to the current debate regarding women's moral voice. Recent works on women's moral discourse[1] and women and moral theory[2] provide questions we can fruitfully ask of Dorothy Day as we seek insight into Day's moral vision and as we ask what her writings might contribute to current debates about women.

For example, what is the language, what the categories Day used to express her religiously informed moral questions, concerns, and approaches to life? Recent discussion about an "ethic of justice" as distinct from an "ethic of care," generated by the empirical studies of

---

1. Carol Gilligan, *In A Different Voice: Psychological Theory and Women's Development*; M. F. Belenky et al., eds., *Women's Ways of Knowing: The Development of Self, Voice, and Mind*; Nel Noddings, *Caring: A Feminine Approach to Ethics and Moral Education*.
2. Eva Feder Kittay and Diana T. Meyers, eds., *Women and Moral Theory*.

50

Lawrence Kohlberg and Carol Gilligan, put us on alert to the place of care and of justice in Day's moral vision and to fundamental experiences of life captured in words such as autonomy and community, individuality and interdependence. Common to ethical discourse is a concern with the source and content of moral principles, the process of moral deliberation, the concept of moral agency. I am interested in the relevance of these themes for understanding Day's moral vision and moral praxis. Less common but nonetheless relevant to ethical reflection is a concern with moral desire and longing, moral aspirations, attitudes, and impulses.[3] I am concerned with these as well, asking in each case how these aspects of living morally can serve as lenses illuminating Dorothy Day's moral vision and how her moral discourse might inform feminist religious ethics.

Day's apologia, *From Union Square to Rome*, reveals her acute moral sensibility. Reflecting on the moral dimensions of the activity of writing itself, Day feels the writer's imperative to be truthful, and yet, because she felt keenly the shifts in perspective that come with the passage of time, she recognized also the impossibility of guaranteeing such a goal.

> I am afraid . . . of not telling the truth or of distorting the truth. I cannot guarantee that I do not for I am writing of the past. But my whole perspective has changed and when I look for causes of my conversion, sometimes it is one thing and sometimes it is another that stands out in my mind. [US, 3]

Since *Union Square* was written not as an autobiography but as a confession and account of her religious faith, Day made no effort to give the full story of her life. Her very purpose enabled her to cite portions of her past briefly, without vivid detail. Early on she alluded to having lived a life of "grievous mortal sin" in her younger years, of having deliberately chosen evil, exhibited arrogance, and pursued a life that she later judged to be "pathetic, little and mean in its very excuse for itself" (US, 2; see also LL, 97).

With this statement, she was, presumably, alluding to her affair with Lionel Moise ("Dick" in *The Eleventh Virgin*) and her brief marriage to Berkeley Tobey.[4] But she chose not to disclose details, for her purpose was more modest: to create a mood of dramatic change so that

---

3. Nel Noddings alerts us to the moral relevance of these categories in her provocative philosophical exploration, *Caring*.
4. William Miller, *Dorothy Day*, 87–199.

the reader would capture something of her own discovery and rediscovery of God. Day would not analyze the concept of conversion. Rather, she assumed its common sense meaning of dramatic change. A widely accepted understanding of conversion as a process that stimulates and reflects a powerful and profound change, a basic transformation of a person's ways of seeing, feeling, valuing, understanding, and relating is useful in studying Day's conversion.[5] Bernard Lonergan underscores the power of conversion by describing it as an "ontic" reality through which the convert apprehends differently from before, values differently, and relates differently, because he or she has become different. New meanings bring new values, indeed, new meanings effect a transvaluation of values.[6] In other words, conversion is much more radical than a change in the content of a faith or life-orientation; it is a change in the structure of one's very outlook. Conversion is constituted by a creative restructuring of questions and meanings, moving one to a more personally reflective apprehension of truth, value, and love, and thus a totally new way of seeing and choosing.[7]

As Day wrote to account for the faith that was in her, she initially attributed her discovery of God to the aloneness she experienced while imprisoned and to her empathy for the poor. She wrote, "always the glimpses of God came most when I was alone. . . . Yet how can I say that either? Better let it be said that I found Him through His poor, and in a moment of joy I turned to Him" (US, 10). Day's reflections on her discovery of God were cast in a searching and exploratory, self-critically reflective and self-corrective mood that brought her far into childhood experiences. She worked her memory to find the key to it all.

One primary memory was the sense of joy she felt at the age of eight, when, after the San Francisco earthquake of 1906, neighbors reached out to aid one another.

What I remember most plainly about the earthquake was the human warmth and kindliness of everyone afterward. . . . Mother and all our neighbors were busy from morning to night cooking hot meals. They gave away every extra garment they possessed. They stripped themselves to the bone in giving, forgetful of the morrow. While the crisis lasted, people loved each other. They

5. Conversion as transformation is characteristic of the writings on conversion by Bernard Lonergan, Walter Conn, Avery Dulles, and Rosemary Haughton. See entries in Bibliography.
6. Bernard Lonergan, "Theology in Its New Context," 55–67.
7. Conn, *Christian Conversion*, 27, 267.

realized their own helplessness while nature "travaileth and groaneth." It was as though they were united in Christian solidarity. [US, 23–24]

Another memory was a sense of beauty as well as joy that was made visible to Dorothy in the person of a neighbor woman on her knees praying. When Dorothy burst into the Barrett apartment, looking for her playmate and friend Kathryn, she found Mrs. Barrett on her knees.

In the front bedroom Mrs. Barrett was on her knees, saying her prayers. She turned to tell me that Kathryn and the children had all gone to the store and went on with her praying. And I felt a warm burst of love toward Mrs. Barrett that I have never forgotten, a feeling of gratitude and happiness that still warms my heart when I remember her. She had God, and there was beauty and joy in her life. [US, 25]

This moment became an enduring memory of meaning and beauty, as the following indicates:

All through my life what she was doing remained with me. And though I became oppressed with the problem of poverty and injustice, though I groaned at the hideous sordidness of man's lot, though there were years when I clung to the philosophy of economic determinism as an explanation of man's fate, still there were moments when in the midst of misery and class strife, life was shot through with glory. Mrs. Barrett in her sordid little tenement flat finished her breakfast dishes at ten o'clock in the morning and got down on her knees and prayed to God. [US, 25]

Dorothy saw special significance also in a childhood moment when a friend read to her the story of some saint. In response she felt a feeling of "lofty enthusiasm" and sensed her heart "almost bursting with desire to take part in such high endeavor" (US, 26). When she found a Bible in the attic of their Berkeley home, Dorothy read it aloud to her sister. She pondered its power:

Slowly, as I read, a new personality impressed itself upon me. I was being introduced to someone and I knew almost immediately that I was discovering God. . . . It was as though life were fuller, richer, more exciting in every way. Here was someone that I had never really known about before and yet felt to be One whom I would never forget, that I would never get away from. The game might grow stale, it might assume new meanings, new aspects, but life would never again be the same. I had made a great discovery. [US, 19]

Nel Noddings's work, *Caring*, alerts us to the importance of memory for both discovering and maintaining ethical ideals. The ethical ideal springs from two sentiments, "the natural sympathy human beings feel for each other and the longing to maintain, recapture or enhance our most caring and tender moments."[8] Dorothy Day's reach into distant childhood experiences of human kindness in the midst of suffering and loss, friendship, the discovery of prayer from a playmate's mother and of the Bible in an attic with her sister alerts us to some of the grounds on which her religious convictions and moral sensibilities were awakened. These tender and caring moments were important not only as warm and happy memories, which they were, but function in Day's memory as moments of religio-ethical significance.[9]

It was Day's adult love for Forster Batterham, however, that in her eyes evoked an enduring sense of the reality and presence of God. Day felt it was the natural love and longing she felt for Forster that opened her to God, nature that brought her to faith (US, 126).

It was human love that helped me to understand divine love. Human love at its best, unselfish, glowing, illuminating our days, gives us a glimpse of the love of God for man. [US, 151]

Because I was grateful for love, I was grateful for life, and living with Forster made me appreciate it and even reverence it still more. He had introduced me to so much that was beautiful and good that I felt I owed to him too this renewed interest in the things of the spirit. [LL, 154]

This, together with her awe at "the stupendous fact of creation" in childbirth, "spiritually and physically a tremendous event" (US, 127), moved Dorothy to worship.

---

8. Noddings, *Caring*, 104.
9. The ethic of caring Noddings displays is based on natural caring. Although Noddings's critical evaluation of religion limits her interest in dealing with it, examining Dorothy Day's ethic of care requires attention to religious sensibilities.

Forster had made the physical world come alive for me and had awakened in my heart a flood of gratitude. The final object of this love and gratitude was God. No human creature could receive or contain so vast a flood of love and joy as I often felt after the birth of my child. With this came the need to worship, to adore.[10] [LL, 159]

Day's falling in love with Forster, together with her earlier feeling of being "in love with the masses" (US, 48), were profoundly influential and lingering experiences, she judged, in her recognition of and receptivity to God.

Influenced by the Marxist views of a professor, Dorothy had dropped religion during her college years. Thus, when she found herself praying after the birth of her child, she felt embarrassed, reminding herself that prayer was the opiate of the people (US, 40–42). The persistence of her desire to pray—prompted by feelings of happiness and gratitude rather than sorrow and emptiness—led Day to trust this instinct to pray, allowing its spontaneous expression and natural development (US, 119–22).

This in turn moved her toward a desire for baptism for Tamar and herself, and with that desire came a feeling of tornness, a wrenching, as she realized this required an end to her family relationship with an unsympathetic Forster. More than a decade later, the intensity of that time remained alive: "These pages are hard to write. The struggle was too personal. It was exceedingly difficult" (US, 141).[11] By the time the separation occurred and the moment for her baptismal ceremony arrived, she apparently operated out of sheer conviction, without any sense of joy, consolation, or peace (US, 141).

---

10. In "Having a Baby," originally published in *New Masses* in 1928, Dorothy described the experience of childbirth in naturalistic terms. Day's flair for vivid description is evident in her portrayal of the process of giving birth as a series of "waves" that became "tidal waves" sweeping over her body. She felt an "earthquake" in her body, "fire" and "lightning," the "rush and the roar of the cataclysm" all about her. After the delivery, she relished Tamar's nursing instincts, describing her as a "lazy little hog, mouthing around my nice full breast." The article ends on an admitted note of complacency, satisfaction, and happiness. Reprinted in *The Catholic Worker*, December 1977, 8, 7 (in that order).

11. A glimpse into the fury of this time in their life is provided in a letter written by Paul Hanley Furfey (department of sociology, Catholic University) to Cardinal O'Connell (archbishop of Boston), 30 October 1935. Cardinal O'Connell requested a response to charges made by a Father Peter Baptist Duffee, O.F.M., about Dorothy Day and her work. Furfey served as intermediary, recording Day's response to the objections made against her. In a letter recounting the circumstances of her common-law marriage and separation and her baptism in the church, Day wrote: "On one occasion he [Forster]

Day brought to her conversion an unconventional morality that was shaped in part by her interests in a Communist workers' revolution together with an attraction to anarchism that sustained itself throughout her life.[12] As a perspective that is critical of all centralized, authoritarian governmental organization, anarchism serves as a critique of the status quo, for in every society there is the effort to exert power over others, to control through institutional structures and the imposed exercise of authority. Anarchism seeks to replace the authoritarian state by some form of nongovernmental cooperation among free individuals.

Anarchism, characterized by an optimistic view of human nature in which it is possible to destroy state authority and yet to maintain society in the free and natural bonds of fraternity, has not succeeded as a historical movement, but it continues to succeed as a critical idea that prods and prompts people to consider and reconsider social arrangements, power, authority, and personal responsibility.[13] The anarchism Day esteemed placed the accent on initiative and personal responsibility. As chapter four will make clear, she stoutly believed that one should not wait to be asked, not wait to be ordered, not wait for permission. One should notice, decide, and act, see a need and meet it. One must not rely on governments, organizations, or institutions to dictate or direct one's judgments and actions.

It is noteworthy that Dorothy's struggle with Forster did not focus on the nonlegal or nonsacramental status of their union. Her conflict, *as she experienced it and articulated it* was far more basic, namely, Forster's repudiation of her interests in religion and in God. These commitments offended his atheist sensibilities and she finally ended the relationship when her health began to break from the tension. When she moved to California and later to Mexico for new work opportunities as a writer, she did so partly because she feared her own desires to return to Forster and needed distance to keep from doing so (LL, 180). The

---

broke into the room where I was staying and tried to choke me to death" (p. 3 of Furfey letter, Dorothy Day-Catholic Worker Archive, Marquette University Library). Subsequent interactions between Dorothy and Forster indicate that they were able to dissolve their hostilities. Day spoke at one point about bringing soup to Forster's wife when she was seriously ill and accounts of Day's funeral tell us that Forster Batterham sat in the front of the church with their daughter Tamar. Years after the separation from Forster, Dorothy still referred to Forster as her husband (Forest, *Love Is the Measure*, 201).

12. For further information on the anarchist features of Day's thought and Catholic worker practice, see Doug Lavine, "Dorothy Day: 40 Years of Works of Mercy"; John Cort, "My Life at the Catholic Worker"; Marc Ellis, *A Year at the Catholic Worker*; Ammon Hennacy, *The Book of Ammon: Autobiography of a Catholic Anarchist*, and Mary Segers, "Equality and Christian Anarchism: The Political and Social Ideas of the Catholic Worker Movement."

13. George Woodcock, *Anarchism: A History of Libertarian Ideas and Movements*, 11, 12.

struggle she endured about this love was not with her church nor its moral precepts (these she never refers to), but with her own sense of realism about the relationship. Day appears to have been working out an authentic personal morality at this time based on her changing interpretations, newly emerging commitments, and realistic judgments. Nothing suggests she was eying an external code to which she felt she must conform. Even in later years, when she voiced a theology of sexuality within marriage, for example, that was in direct agreement with traditional Catholic sexual teachings, her support for her position was rooted not in the church's authority as such but in what she judged to be the wisdom of a viewpoint that she had arrived at from painful direct experience (OPS, 159; OP, 63).

From the point of view of her marriage, Dorothy's conversion rendered her alone. Yet in spite of membership in her new community, she felt alone in the church as well. She had been impressed with the large masses of poor, largely immigrant peoples who filled the city churches when she went to Mass. But a radical anarchist Catholic was surely a rarity. If there were others, their anarchist preferences and inclinations would have made them inaccessible to each other. She had no Catholic friends and many of her Communist friends felt that her conversion put a barrier between them (LL, 184). And given her sense of identification with workers throughout the world, she had difficulty shaking the feeling that she was betraying her class by becoming a Catholic (US, 138–39). Although she was close to her sister Della throughout her life, neither Della nor others in Dorothy's family shared her Catholic vision. Her feelings of loneliness were surely compounded by a sense of aloneness endemic to being a single working parent of a young child.

The critical eye toward conventional morality that characterized Day as a young adult accompanied her into her church; she used that critical view to critique conventional Christianity and American Catholicism as well as American society more generally. Day was less than enthusiastic about the Catholic school system, for example, with its preoccupations with fund-raising and building projects. She urged city pastors to open up houses of hospitality within the parish community and not merely refer the destitute to Catholic Worker houses. She noted the comfort of the clergy and convent living, as she argued for voluntary poverty. She accepted without question persons of every religious persuasion and of no religious inclination long before ecumenism became a part of the American Catholic landscape.

One might well wonder how this anarchist felt about and related to the authoritative structures so characteristic of the Roman Catholic tradition. To what extent was her conversion one in which she took responsibility for the meanings she appropriated, the understandings she processed, and the judgments she came to? Or was she uncritically accepting of her church's authority?

With respect to theological and doctrinal matters, Dorothy Day was seemingly uncritical; in that sphere she deferred readily and easily.

Without even looking into the claims of the Catholic Church, I was willing to admit that for me she was the one true Church. She had come down through the centuries since the time of Peter, and far from being dead, she claimed and held the allegiance of the masses of people in all the cities where I had lived. They poured in and out of her doors on Sundays and holy days, for novenas and missions. What if they were compelled to come in by the law of the Church, which said they were guilty of mortal sin if they did not go to Mass every Sunday? They obeyed that law. They were given a chance to show their preference. They accepted the Church. It may have been an unthinking, unquestioning faith, and yet the chance certainly came, again and again, "Do I prefer the Church to my own will," even if it was only the small matter of sitting at home on a Sunday morning with the papers? And the choice was the Church. [LL, 159–60]

Dorothy's criteria for credibility were the church's age and continuity through history together with the affection and loyalty for the church which she observed in the urban immigrant masses.

Day was not interested in "doing" philosophical or historical theology nor in eying critically doctrinal teachings and formulations. This lack of interest sustained itself throughout her life; in this respect she was decidedly (for she had decided to be) uncritical, exempting herself from an area of inquiry in which she was never trained and apparently had no desire to train herself. An intensely practical person, Dorothy Day had little interest in the metaphysical speculation and philosophical debates that characterized the theology she inherited. She held no great esteem for personal autonomy as distinct from or in competition with external authority. She trusted the masses more than she trusted the single individual self. Her judgments were formed reflectively and deliberatively in relation and response to a community of people she loved and trusted.

This is not to say that her judgments were not her own. Dorothy Day had great interest in moral reflection and persuasion; her writings exhibit neither diffidence nor reliance on others for her moral judgments. For all her rhetoric of deference to "the Church," it is notable that she exhibited no reluctance in disagreeing with the church's officers, not only for not living up to the demands of the gospel (US, 15), but also with respect to the issues of just war and conscientious objection. As chapter four discusses in greater detail, her insistence on the rightness of pacifism and the moral appropriateness of conscientious objection in response to Pope Pius XII's 1956 Christmas message (which supported a doctrine of just war and criticized conscientious objector status for Catholics) illustrated her willingness publicly to voice her convictions however unofficial or unpopular.[14] Yet she also made it clear that she "didn't become a Catholic in order to purify the church."[15] The church was her home, not her forum for effecting change:

> I didn't ever see myself as posing a challenge to church authority. . . . I have not wanted to challenge the church . . . on any of its doctrinal positions.[16] I try to be loyal to the church—to its teachings, its ideals. I love the church with all my heart and soul. I never go inside a church without thanking God Almighty for giving me a home. The church *is* my home, and I don't want to be homeless. I may work with the homeless, but I have had no desire to join their ranks.[17]

Absenting herself in these ways from theological and doctrinal debates, Day preferred to participate in discussions regarding morality, spirituality, and social policy; through these she exposed and discussed the values of pacifism and voluntary poverty, fair wages and working arrangements, the practice of the spiritual and corporal works of mercy.

Day's feeling of oneness with others predated her Christian conversion and may be the key to understanding and assessing her contribution to our understanding of the moral life. As a young radical, Dorothy sensed and felt within her the experience, the pain, even the horror of others in a remarkably empathetic manner. Her sense of

---

14. Day, "On Pilgrimage," *The Catholic Worker*, January 1957, 2.

15. Coles, *Radical Devotion*, 86.

16. In a 1937 paper in which Dorothy answered some charges placed against the Catholic Worker, she voiced a distinction which served her throughout her life's work: matters of faith and doctrine were matters to be handled by the church's officers, but "our convictions along economic and sociological lines, those are matters of opinion, to be threshed out in the paper" (D-7, no. 1, p. 2, Dorothy Day-Catholic Worker Collection, Marquette University Library).

17. Coles, *Radical Devotion*, 82.

oneness extended even to those with socially reprehensible behaviors. Early prison reflections demonstrate this sensibility well:

> I was no longer a young girl, part of a radical movement seeking justice for those oppressed, I was the oppressed. I was that drug addict, screaming and tossing in her cell, beating her head against the wall. I was that shoplifter who for rebellion was sent to solitary. I was that woman who had killed her children, who had murdered her lover. . . . I was that mother whose child had been raped and slain. I was the mother who had borne the monster who had done it. I was even that monster, feeling in my own heart every abomination. [US, 6]

I was, I was, I was . . . the drug addict, the mother-murderer, the mother of the victim of rape, the mother of the rapist-monster, the monster-rapist himself. Day empathized with all of these players in the tragic and destructive dramas of life. While for some, conversion to God brings with it a feeling of oneness with others, Day's experience was quite the opposite. Her feeling of oneness with others stimulated her religious conversion.

A long-term and deep-seated love for the masses and empathy for the poor and the destitute became charged with the imagery of the Mystical Body of Christ. Her reflections on the 23 August 1927 execution of Nicola Sacco and Bartolomeo Vanzetti and the sense of solidarity Day and her friends felt with the two men demonstrate the way in which her conversion brought a new sense of meaning:

> While enjoying the fresh breeze, the feel of salt water against the flesh, the keen delight of living, the knowledge that these men were soon to pass from this physical earth, were soon to become dust, without consciousness, struck me like a physical blow. They were here now; in a few days they would be no more. They had become figures beloved by the workers. Their letters, the warm moving story of their lives, had been told. Everyone knew Dante, Sacco's young son. Everyone suffered with the young wife who clung with bitter passion to her husband. And Vanzetti with his large view, his sense of peace at his fate, was even closer to us all.
>
> The day they died, the papers had headlines as large as those which proclaimed the outbreak of war. All the nation mourned. All the nation, that is, that is made up of the poor, the worker, the trade unionist,—those who felt most keenly the sense of solidarity,—that very sense of solidarity which made me gradually

understand the doctrine of the Mystical Body of Christ whereby we are the members one of another.[18] [US, 140]

Day's long-grounded social commitments became newly appreciated in religious terms and newly justified on religious grounds. Day adopted and adapted the metaphor of the body of Christ, rooted in the New Testament and particularly evident in early twentieth-century Roman Catholic teachings,[19] to advance her work on behalf of the poor. The doctrine of the Mystical Body supported, deepened, enhanced, and beautified an ethic of caring which she had committed herself to years earlier.

Discussion about the moral language of caring has recently stimulated a debate about an "ethic of care" as distinct from an "ethic of justice," prompted by the social scientific research of Lawrence Kohlberg and Carol Gilligan. Since Kohlberg's widely accepted and much discussed theory of moral development makes universalizable judgments about moral growth and development and since his research is based on work with men and boys, Gilligan wishes to make explicit the gender-specific features of his research and thus the limitations of his conclusions.[20]

Gilligan's own research on moral decision-making based on samples of women prompts her to identify an ethic of care as characteristic of the women she studied as distinct from an ethic of justice which characterizes the ethic Kohlberg claims to describe. The ethic of justice is marked by a concern for justice as the preeminent moral virtue and by a concern for rights and rules, fairness and equality as categories central for dealing with mature moral decision-making. The ethic of care is marked by a concern for care as the fundamental moral virtue

---

18. The July-August 1977 issue of *The Catholic Worker* was dedicated to the memory of Sacco and Vanzetti. An article by Robert Ellsberg ("Sacco and Vanzetti") in that issue cites the anniversary of their death as a reminder of the greatness of human beings, their depth of feeling, and their profound generosity and loyalty to an idea they believed in (p. 1). He raises their memory also as a stimulus to critically examine the return of the death penalty in the United States.

On the fiftieth anniversary of their execution, 23 August 1977, the governor of Massachusetts exonerated Sacco and Vanzetti and cleared their names.

19. For example, Fulton Sheen, *The Mystical Body of Christ* (New York: Sheed and Ward, 1935); Emile Mersch, *The Theology of the Mystical Body*, trans. Cyril Vollert (St. Louis, MO: Herder, 1952); Pope Pius XII, *Mystici Corporis*.

20. See Lawrence Kohlberg, *The Philosophy of Moral Development*, *The Psychology of Moral Development*, and "Moral Stages and Moralization," for selected works. See also Carol Gilligan, *In a Different Voice*, "Moral Orientation and Moral Development," and *Mapping the Moral Domain*.

and a concern for relationships and responsibilities-in-relation as central issues for discerning wise and good moral judgment.

Attention to the moral dimension of Dorothy Day's religious conversion challenges us to find categories that respect both her passion for justice and her commitments to care. Because Day publicly voiced her support of the laborer, the Cuban revolution, the anti-Vietnam War movement, the civil rights movement, and the farm workers' campaign, and because she frequently marched, picketed, civilly disobeyed, and endured imprisonment on behalf of these movements, it is tempting to say that she was a woman with a passion for justice who put her body on the line. But I find it noteworthy that the language of justice with its emphasis on rights, rules, fairness, and equality is not prominent in her writings. In its stead, we find descriptions of human suffering and diminishment accompanied by the language of love, care, and an invitation to those on the margins of the social order to participate in her community's endeavors.

Gilligan's more recent discussions[21] make clear that in the ethic of care and ethic of justice debate we are faced with two "moral perspectives" or "moral orientations." Care and justice are not identical; they are not opposites. Nor are they "mirror-images of each other, with justice uncaring and care unjust."[22] Instead, these perspectives denote different ways of envisioning the relationship between self and others, which are the basic elements of moral judgment. Where the justice perspective sees the relationship in terms of inequality and equality, the care perspective focuses on attachment and detachment. Thoughts, feelings, and language shift so that words connoting relationship, such as dependence and responsibility, and moral terms like fairness and care, take on different meanings. To envision relationships in terms of attachment rather than equality alters images of connectedness. While a justice/equality perspective suggests images of judicial balance and ordered hierarchy, a care/attachment perspective suggests network or web.[23] Dorothy Day's preferred metaphor was the body of Christ, wherein people are seen in their connectedness, as interdependent members of a greater whole. When one is injured the whole body hurts, when one is healed the whole body feels better. In Day's moral vision,

---

21. Gilligan, "Moral Orientation and Moral Development," in Kittay and Meyers, eds., *Women and Moral Theory*, 19–33; see also *Mapping the Moral Domain.*
22. Gilligan, "Moral Orientation and Moral Development," 22.
23. From a justice perspective, the self as moral agent stands as the figure against a ground of social relationships, judging the conflicting claims of self and others against a standard of equality or equal respect (the Categorical Imperative, the Golden Rule). From a care perspective, the relationship becomes the figure, defining self and others. See n. 21 above.

the "attachment" denotations of the body of Christ included relationship to God as well as the relations of human persons to one another.

Day's appeal to others to share her vision was not cast in terms of justice and rights as much as it was cast in terms of dignity, respect, and love for the brother and sister whose keeper she believed she was. In the justice view, the accent is placed on the self as self with efforts placed on respect for and rights due the self. In the care orientation, the accent is placed on the self-in-relation and on the responsiveness which relational existence elicits. Both senses of self are grounded in experience (we are indeed both individual and social beings), yet each reflects a distinctive way of naming experience. Dorothy Day's moral discourse expresses an unyielding belief in the relationships all persons have with one another. She clearly preferred to be and work with the poor, directing her energies to the marginalized, the underprivileged, and the needy. They were, she judged, in greatest need of attention, kindness, and assistance because in their suffering and pain they had fewer resources than the privileged and little or no social power, knowledge, or skills to draw upon. She focused on those who were without: without money, housing, food, power, knowledge, talents, skills, and luck; but also, often enough, persons without gratitude, courtesy, desire, hope, or fundamental likability. What they needed, above all, were kindness and opportunities to participate in the social order; Day cooked, served, wrote, and marched for these purposes. The principle she appealed to in making moral judgments was a commitment grounded in empathy for the poor whom she met in San Francisco, Chicago, New York, Conyers and Americus, Georgia, and Fresno, California. Her religious sensibilities, based on gospel values and informed by the social encyclicals together with the thought of Thomas Aquinas, Jacques Maritain, Hilaire Belloc, G. K. Chesterton, Eric Gill, Vincent McNabb, Emmanuel Mounier, among others, enhanced and deepened this natural attraction.

Nel Noddings's interest in ethics and moral analysis is particularly pertinent to a study of Dorothy Day because Noddings's primary attention is given not to moral reasoning nor moral judgments as found in the justice perspective, but rather on *how we meet the other morally*.[24] This focus—how we meet the other morally—I believe, penetrates Dorothy Day's distinctive moral vision and contribution. Caring is the *foundation* of this ethic which Noddings seeks to voice, not merely a manifestation of it. Recognition of relatedness and the human longing for relatedness constitute its base; joy is seen as the basic human affect

---

24. Noddings, *Caring*, 5.

sustaining and enhancing this longing. Noddings raises issues that invite debate. She claims, for example, that

> the impulse to act in behalf of the present other is itself innate. It lies latent in each of us, awaiting gradual development in a succession of caring relations. . . . but we are not compelled by this impulse. We have a choice; we may accept what we feel, or we may reject it. If we have a strong desire to be moral, we will not reject it, and this strong desire to be moral is derived, reflectively, from the more fundamental and natural desire to be and to remain related. To reject the feeling when it arises is either to be in an internal state of imbalance or to contribute willfully to the diminution of the ethical ideal.[25]

Although claims such as these about the nature of things are apt subjects for debate, I wish simply to note that Noddings's position (together with Gilligan and the many others who have joined in discussion[26]) alerts us to avenues of thought characteristic of Dorothy Day that may well assist us in understanding her moral vision and the distinctiveness of her moral voice.

Noddings's description of the one-caring is an apt portrayal of Day: one who is characterized by a readiness to bestow, to be available, to be present. Noddings's view of caring highlights attitudes and dispositions of receptivity and responsiveness to others. Furthermore, an "ethic of caring locates morality primarily in the pre-act consciousness of the one-caring."[27] Earlier in this chapter we noted that Dorothy Day's life story located the origins of that pre-act consciousness in feelings recovered from childhood memories—the joy of neighborly charity in response to the San Francisco earthquake (US, 23–24), enthusiasm for spiritual adventure (US, 26), shock at the conditions and the smell of poverty (LL, 58).

Dorothy Day's story is marked by strong, intense, and memorable feelings. More importantly, I have come to see, her story illustrates the

25. Noddings, *Caring*, 83.
26. In the Kittay and Meyers volume, *Women and Moral Theory*, see the editors' "Introduction" and the following essays: Michael Stocker, "Duty and Friendship: Toward a Synthesis of Gilligan's Contrastive Moral Concepts"; Virginia Held, "Feminism and Moral Theory"; Thomas E. Hill, Jr., "The Importance of Autonomy"; George Sher, "Other Voices, Other Rooms? Women's Psychology and Moral Theory"; Sandra Harding, "The Curious Coincidence of Feminine and African Moralities." See also Jean Grimshaw, *Feminist Philosophers: Women's Perspectives on Philosophical Traditions*.
27. Noddings, *Caring*, 29.

moral relevance of feelings and the centrality of feeling in the construction of a moral vision. If we take Noddings's recommendation seriously, we will expand the current emphasis on moral reasoning and the analysis of moral judgments to include those more hidden, difficult-to-get-at sources of moral vision and moral action such as feelings, longings, impulses, and desires, utilizing categories not commonly scrutinized in ethical debate. An ethic of care, Noddings tells us, is not a matter of projecting, as is connoted in the image of putting oneself in the shoes of the other; it is a matter of reception rather than projection, of receiving the other into oneself, based on a desire to see as and to feel with the other. An example: to care for a child who hates mathematics, she warns, is not first of all to say to oneself, "I must help this poor boy to love mathematics." It is, first and foremost, to say to oneself, "How would it feel to hate mathematics?"[28] Day's concern for the famous and the anonymous, for Sacco, Vanzetti, Julius and Ethel Rosenberg, for the Japanese at Hiroshima, and the destitute on Mott, Chrystie, and Third streets in New York illustrate again and again a marked capacity as well as a desire to feel as others feel.

While feeling is not all that is involved in an act of caring, it is essentially involved, for *ethical feeling precedes ethical knowing*. The mother's response to the crying infant becomes Noddings's model for ethics: one begins by sharing a feeling, not by formulating a problem; by feeling with before claiming to know about.[29] Day's identification with the drug addict, shoplifter, murderer, and rapist seems best uncovered and understood by utilizing a moral perspective that takes seriously empathy, receptivity, and identification with others. For part of Day's distinctive contribution to moral reflection and moral living seems to lie in her capacity to see others in herself and herself in others.[30] A two-week stay in a Fresno area jail with California migrant workers in 1973, for example, led Day to meditate about the inconveniences and indignities that had characterized the Japanese-American internment camps decades earlier and the burdens felt by agricultural workers as a whole. As reporter and editor, she then brought these

---

28. Noddings, *Caring*, 19.
29. Noddings, *Caring*, 34–35.
30. I have highlighted Day's capacity for empathizing and identifying with others. It is worth noting, however, that Day assumed that others could also identify with her, particularly in her identity as woman, mother, and grandmother. Writing from West Virginia where she was helping her daughter with a new baby and young children, she stated that since her family was like all families she would speak in terms of "I" and "mine" and in doing so, readers would feel "it is their own hopes and fears and joys and sorrows they are reading about, common to us all" (OP,5).

historical facts and social conditions to the attention of her readers.[31] Dorothy Day's ethic is an ethic of personal care and social critique grounded in the values of justice and the will to love. By connecting her experience with the experience of other persons and communities in distant decades and places, Day sought to inform and arouse the conscience of her readers, urging them to engage in direct action.

31. Day, "On Pilgrimage," *The Catholic Worker*, January 1977, 1, 6.

4

THE RADICAL:
ON POWER, POVERTY, AND
PACIFISM

DOROTHY DAY'S SELF-UNDERSTANDING AS A RADICAL endured
throughout her life. Although the revolutionary consciousness she
found compelling in her twenties was modified, due to her conversion,
with a shift from a Communist world view to a Catholic Christian world
view, an underlying continuity between these two historical periods and
these competing world views can be seen in her ethical concerns and
commitments. In both contexts, Dorothy was drawn to work for radical
social change. As a Catholic Worker she considered herself one of a
community of "revolutionaries who are encouraged in trying to build a
new social order" (HH, 239) marked by anarchism, pacifism, and the
works of mercy. This ambitious goal brought her into conflict with the
giant power of the state, with her chosen church, and even with her
Catholic Worker associates.

Understandings of power and expressions of power are of particular interest to feminist thinkers who seek to analyze societies in
which power is a highly prized social value and fundamental means of
ordering social arrangements. Marilyn French presses all of us to consider how power is to be understood—whether chiefly as control or
domination, on the one hand, or as an ability or capacity, a freedom, on
the other hand.[1]

---

1. French, *Beyond Power: On Women, Men, and Morals.*

67

Others press us to consider whether our assumed or consciously preferred views about power are essentially coercive or cooperative, dominating or empowering, and whether power itself is better understood as an attribute or as a process shared by parties, at least one of whom, by allowing the other(s) to exercise power, holds power.[2] Internal debate among feminists urges examination of the extent to which the models of strength by which many feminists have named and valued power are based on the partial and limited experience of middle-class women. In this context, the power envisioned and wanted is grounded in the confidence and self-determination that characterize white, middle-class men.[3] Elizabeth Janeway leads us (all, feminists and non-feminists alike) to consider the "powers of the weak."[4] Elise Boulding alerts readers to ways women might bring their "underside" experience, and the skills developed there, to the "overside" of history as they participate more fully in the public sphere.[5]

Given Dorothy Day's identity as a social radical, I find it useful to probe her understanding of power by allowing the discussions cited to accompany my examination of her thought and actions and by asking what she might contribute about this issue to women's moral discourse today. How did she envision and exercise power within her own Catholic Worker community? Did Day enjoy power? Did she encourage others to share her power or to express their own? Was she coercive or cooperative, dictatorial or empowering in style? On what grounds does her approach to power, use of power, and response to power reside? As a member of the powerful international Roman Catholic church, how did Dorothy Day relate to ecclesial power? As an American activist and social protestor, in what ways did she deal with social, political, and economic forces with which she often stood in disagreement and dissent? To probe these questions I wish to envision Dorothy Day in three settings and sets of relationships: the state, the church, and her Catholic Worker community.

Dorothy Day and the State

On nearly a dozen occasions, between 1917 and 1973, Dorothy "did time." As a result of her protesting the holding of political prisoners (during the suffrage campaigns), mandatory public air raid drills,

---

2. Nancy Hartsock, "Political Change: Two Perspectives on Power"; Gene Sharp has an excellent discussion of power in *The Politics of Nonviolent Action*.

3. Karen Kollias, "Class Realities: Create a New Power Base"; Bell Hooks, *Feminist Theory: From Margin to Center* and *Ain't I a Woman: Black Women and Feminism*; Angela Davis, *Women, Race, and Class*.

4. Elizabeth Janeway, *Powers of the Weak*.

5. Elise Boulding, *The Underside of History: A View of Women Through Time*.

unfair, unsafe working conditions for California farm workers, American involvement in World War II and in Vietnam, Dorothy was imprisoned—for hours, days, or weeks. Vigils, pickets, strikes, marches, boycotts, advocacy journalism, speaking and publishing, as well as imprisonment, were vehicles of protest which she regarded as "spiritual works of mercy"—ways of instructing the ignorant, persuading the thoughtful, indoctrinating the open-minded, and always arousing the conscience. She saw no reason for leaving the streets to the Communists and the Salvation Army; she longed for fellow Catholics and others to join her.

An episode from 15 June 1955, when the government's air raid wardens required citizens to take shelter at the sound of the sirens, provides an example.

> Just before two p.m. we went to the park and sat down on the benches there, and when the sirens began their warning we continued to sit. That was all there was to it. A number of elaborately uniformed men with much brass, stars and ribbons of past battles hung upon their blue auxiliary police outfits marched upon us and told us to move. When we refused, they announced we were under arrest, and the police van was driven up inside the park, up over the curb and we were loaded in and driven away.

Anticipating her readers' questions, Day provides a threefold rationale for her actions:

> We make this demonstration, not only to voice our opposition to war, not only to refuse to participate in psychological warfare, which this air-raid drill is, but also as an act of public penance for having been the first people in the world to drop the atom bomb, to make the hydrogen bomb.[6]

Day was jailed four times for resisting in this fashion on at least six occasions between 1955 and 1960.[7] Her disapproval of war was rooted in the common-sense recognition that war is the opposite of the works of mercy. Wars destroy land, separate, diminish, and kill people, nourish enmity and suspicion, and aggrandize self-righteousness. Her pacifist convictions were supported by the Sermon on the Mount and her sense

---

6. Day, "Where Are the Poor? They Are in Prisons, Too."
7. William Miller, *A Harsh and Dreadful Love: Dorothy Day and the Catholic Worker Movement*, 283–86; see also Dorothy Day, "Vocation to Prison."

of felt connection with people of every nation, race, and region. She counseled young men to resist conscription and supported imprisonment or conscientious objector status as preferred alternatives.

As a woman, Day felt self-conscious being so strong about an issue which would never threaten her as it would touch and challenge men. Thus she mused in one entry what she would do if conscription came for women. Should such a thing occur, Day would not only refuse to register as those who knew her might expect; she would refuse also, she wrote, to make a statement explaining her stand lest this action be interpreted as involuntary registration. She would not register, she explains, because "I believe modern war to be murder, incompatible with a religion of love. . . . the only way to do away with war is to do away with conscription."[8]

Anticipating questions from her readers—why does she object to registering? why not go ahead and register and then refuse to serve if called?—she answered, "By little and by little we must resist. Why take the first step if we do not intend to go on? Why . . . lose the opportunity to testify to the truth that we feel so strongly?"[9]

Other forms of protest to the state (which she sardonically referred to as "Holy Mother State") included returning a check to the city of New York in 1960 for $3,579.39 since it represented interest on the Catholic Worker Chrystie Street property. Dorothy Day felt that interest and financial investments, money making money, were fundamentally wrong.[10] The only investments she believed in were human actions such as creating housing for the poor or creating work opportunities—not just created work, but genuinely needed services.[11]

What some observers might have read as a sense of drama, expression of purist attitudes, or poor judgment regarding money was for Day an opportunity to witness to the truth and value as she saw it, an opportunity to make known her views on issues of conscience. The hopes and motivations pervading these protest activities were vividly captured in an expression influenced by Ignazio Silone's *Bread and Wine*: "One person shouting 'no' is enough to break the unanimity."[12] No to the absurdity of air raid drills; no to money contaminated by a system of interest she found exploitative and unjust; no to conscription; no to war. Even one person shouting no would be enough to break the

---

8. Day, "If Conscription Comes for Women."
9. Day, "If Conscription Comes for Women."
10. Day, "This Money Is Not Ours."
11. See Dean Brackley and Dennis Dillon, "An Interview with Dorothy Day."
12. Jim Wallis and Wes Michaelson, "Dorothy Day: Exalting Those of Low Degree," 18.

unanimity. As horrible as jail was,[13] it was a price worth paying. "We protest in any way we can, according to our responsibilities and temperaments."[14]

This deep-seated readiness to protest led her to empathize in a particularly interesting way with Ethel and Julius Rosenberg who, for two years in a death house, were "watched without ceasing so [much so] that there [was] no chance of one taking one's life, and *so thwarting the vengeance of the State*."[15] This quotation illustrates anew the radical quality of Day's thought. Through nonviolent resistance activities, Day utilized the power of noncooperation in order to render ineffective the commanding powers of state authority. Integral to these acts of resistance was Day's esteem for voluntary poverty which she found a freeing force enabling her to speak out and follow the ideals of conscience. Owning nothing, she had nothing to lose and thus greater freedom to act. Voluntary poverty provided opportunities to show solidarity with the poor, to live in tune with her conscience and, through noncooperation, to refuse to participate in evil. She extended her resistance activities toward the state to her church as well.

Dorothy Day and the Church

When Pope Pius XII distributed his 23 December 1956 Christmas message, citing with approval the conditions for a just war and disapproving the stance of the conscientious objector, phone calls and letters poured in to editor Day, asking her reaction. The pope's letter had outlined the justifiability of war in terms of the classic conditions: (1) "after every effort to avoid war has been expended in vain," (2) "for effective self-defense," (3) "by legitimate instruments of internal and external policy," and (4) "with the hope of a favorable outcome against unjust attack." His conclusion: "Therefore a Catholic citizen cannot invoke his own conscience in order to refuse to serve and fulfill those duties the law imposes."[16]

Dorothy Day's response was of interest to many, given the Catholic Worker stand in support of conscientious objection and given her Roman Catholic identity and loyalties. In the January 1957 issue of *The Catholic Worker*, Dorothy summarized the pope's statement of support

---

13. Day, "Have You Ever Been to Jail," 5.
14. Day, "CW Refuses Tax Exemption," 1.
15. Day, "Meditation on the Death of the Rosenbergs" (leaflet), 2 (emphasis added).
16. "The Contradiction of Our Age," *The Pope Speaks*, 343.

according to the just war tradition's conditions and criteria. She then stated simply, "but we continue to take the stand that it is impossible for these conditions to be fulfilled."[17] In a series of rhetorical questions, editor Day drove home her point: All other means must have been used; have we used them? Has war in Hungary or the Near East or in Egypt been declared by duly constituted authority? Is there probability of success in the satellite countries fighting against an armed Russia? She then reminded her readers that since the pope reiterated his call for disarmament in the course of his message, she "cannot feel that he is calling for war, or endorsing war, as so many are trying to make it appear he is doing."[18]

She disagreed with the pope's position in that he allowed for the possibility of justifiable war; Dorothy judged that in real, historical wars, these conditions are never met and that in modern war, since 1945, they cannot be met. People fight for revenge and retaliation, domination of land and peoples, without duly constituted authority to support them, before all other means of resolution have been tried, and in an atomic age with a meaningless concept of hope for success.

On matters of substance, her disagreement with the pope was clear, yet she never named her response one of disagreement or dissent. Rather, she employed a literary strategy, the rhetorical question, to provoke her readers' thought about this matter, citing historical example to demonstrate her point. Furthermore, she found a common platform in the pope's call for disarmament, a goal she shared. Focusing on disarmament, she alerted her readers to the fact that because the pope hoped for disarmament, he could not possibly be understood to be endorsing or encouraging war.

Dorothy Day's disagreement with Francis Cardinal Spellman of New York had been more direct. In 1949 the church's cemetery workers began to strike. The cardinal referred to the strike as "anti-American, anti-Christian evil," and "a strike against the Church." But Dorothy supported the strikers, telling them that their action was Christian and that they themselves were the church.[19] She knew the Catholic position that the authority of the church's officers pertained only to faith and morals and that judgments about social systems and economic strategies were matters of opinion. Her opinion supporting the strikers became public record as did the cardinal's condemnation of the action.

In later years, she told an interviewer her thinking at the time.

17. Day, "On Pilgrimage," *The Catholic Worker*, January 1957, 2.
18. Day, "On Pilgrimage," *The Catholic Worker*, January 1957, 2.
19. Milton Mayer, "God's Panhandler," 14.

The Catholic Church *is* authoritarian in a way; it won't budge on what it believes it has been put here to protect and defend and uphold. But the church has never told its flock that they have no rights of their own, that they ought to have no beliefs or loyalties other than those of the pope or one of his cardinals. No one in the church can tell me what to think about social and political and economic questions without getting a tough speech back: please leave me alone and tend to your own acreage; I'll take care of mine.[20]

Indeed, if the cardinal had ordered the Catholic Worker to shut down its operations (as some feared he might very well do because of the Worker's radical politics and in spite of its admirable works of mercy for the poor), Dorothy would have picketed and protested that abuse of power as well.

We were ready to go to Saint Patrick's, fill up the church, stand outside it, in prayerful meditation. We were ready to take advantage of America's freedoms so that we could say what we thought and do what we believed was the right thing to do.[21]

Confrontation with the cardinal of her beloved church was for Day an emotionally, psychologically, and theologically live option. With the pope, Day utilized critical reflection and analysis to express her difference of opinion and to stimulate the thinking of her readers; with the cardinal of New York she stood prepared to engage in silent, prayerful confrontation. With the bishop of San Diego, she employed yet a third strategy: simply ignoring the officer of the church and going about her intentions without confrontation or concession. Every time she went to San Diego to speak, she recorded, the bishop of San Diego cancelled the meeting.

Some sisters would invite me and suddenly the meeting would be cancelled. Some priests would invite me to their parish, the meeting would be cancelled. And then we would just go to the house of a lay person and have a meeting and the priests would come there. . . . We went ahead, we spoke in his diocese; we had good meetings there. It didn't keep us from expressing ourselves and it didn't keep the priests from coming to the meetings either.[22]

---

20. Coles, *Radical Devotion*, 83.
21. Coles, *Radical Devotion*, 84.
22. Day, "Fear in Our Time" (Pax Conference, Spode House), 14–15.

The bishop sent the Catholic Worker a two hundred dollar check after one meeting, which some interpreted as "conscience money" but which Dorothy interpreted as approval by the bishop of their just going ahead without asking permission, without involving him. She criticized the "Dear Father" mentality among many Catholics which she felt seriously limited and constricted people who wanted priests and bishops to endorse and approve every action they took. She cleverly turned the cancellation of her speech into an affirmation of her initiative.

> . . . I would say that the clergy should be very happy and probably are very happy that we are instigating a movement among the laity of going ahead on our own. Why should we go ahead and wait until we have dear Father come to our meetings[?] It is impossible to say how much that has limited the activity of the Church.[23]

Clearly co-optation by way of compliment, in contrast to concession or confrontation, was the strategy for the moment. In this way, Day not only exercised her intent to speak, but provided the interpretation that good common sense, together with the bishop's financial donation, indicated support for the initiatives she took and encouraged in others. After all, she reasoned, such initiatives were a freedom for the clergy: a freedom from having to approve in advance and thus bear responsibility for the actions of the laity.

The sense of optimism and feeling of personal affirmation expressed in this episode with church authority took quite a different turn when Dorothy Day visited the Vatican in 1963 as one of more than fifty Mothers for Peace—an international group of Catholic Workers, Pax Christi members, Women's International League for Peace and Freedom, Fellowship of Reconciliation members, and others, from the United States, South America, Asia, and Europe (OPS, 141). Their purpose, in Dorothy's eyes, was clear: to thank Pope John XXIII for his letter on peace, *Pacem in Terris*, to pledge themselves to work for peace, and *to ask for a more radical condemnation of the instruments of modern warfare* than he had given to date (OPS, 137). She was greatly disappointed that neither she nor the others were allowed to

---

23. Day, "Fear in Our Time," 15. Twenty years later, Dorothy Day would be singled out by the American Roman Catholic bishops as an admirable witness to Christian pacifism whose work had a profound impact on the life of the Church in the United States ("The Challenge of Peace," 1983, par. 117).

speak to the pope directly, and observed in a column of *The Catholic Worker* that "it is no easier to receive a hearing with Princes of the Church than it is to receive one from the princes of this world" (OPS, 144). She found "hierarchy," "protocol," and "blocs of one kind or another" in the Vatican's ways of doing things. These difficulties were compounded by the "maneuvering" for credit and nationalist recognition among the women themselves (OPS, 144).

As she climbed onto the bus that would take the women to the Vatican for the huge papal audience in St. Peter's Square, Dorothy registered surprise that the women's group was being handled in the same way as the visiting school children (gathered from all over Europe to visit the Vatican during a holiday). When the general audience finally occurred (a private audience which the women had hoped for was not permitted), numerous groups of pilgrims were identified, but the Mothers for Peace were not mentioned. Dorothy was stunned and saddened. Why had their pilgrimage not been officially received? Dorothy pressed this question only to be given the explanation by an American priest in Rome, that it was believed that communists were a part of the group Day was with. After a one hour interview with Cardinal Bea in which she pressed her concerns about a more developed ecclesial position on the morality and theology of war and peace in the modern world, Day left. Her conclusion: "that the clergy did not know too much about any lay movements in the world that questioned either the injustices of the social order by direct action, or that tried to educate the people in the ways of peace" through refusal of conscription, refusal to pay taxes for war, use of nonviolence in racial struggles, and voluntary poverty. She "came away from Rome more convinced than ever that the particular vocation of *The Catholic Worker* is to reach the man in the street" (OPS, 148). She was allowed no personal presentation, no possibility for serious, mutual argumentation. Even her interview with Cardinal Bea offered no serious response to her position but deferred discussion of such matters to the council chambers of Vatican II. In the United States, Dorothy was a presence to be reckoned with and she had more than a few opportunities to make her positions known to the officers of her church. In Rome she was voiceless and she knew it. That was an audience she would not take on.[24] She returned to New York recommitting herself to the "man in the street." But home had its conflicts, too.

---

24. For alternative responses to church authority, see Mary Jo Weaver, *New Catholic Women: Contemporary Challenge to Traditional Religious Authority*, and Ann Patrick Ware, "Change and Confrontation within the Roman Catholic Church."

Dorothy Day and the Catholic Worker Community

At home, Day's voice was listened to and reckoned with. As founder of the Catholic Worker movement and publisher of its paper, she served as the functional authority in the community. Insight into the sort of authority she held and the kind of power she expressed is best gleaned from those who worked and lived in the community, together with Dorothy's own writings. John Cort records a reminiscence that discloses Day's leadership position and style. Weary of the bedbugs and dirt in the Worker house, Cort took it upon himself to post three typewritten rules for his companions, who consisted of both Workers and guests. Rule one required everyone to be out of bed by 9 A.M. Rule two that each man make his own bed. Rule three that each take turns sweeping up. One of the guests ("a Bowery type") objected, appealing to Dorothy to support his objection that these rules violated the principles of personalism that Dorothy stood for. Dorothy agreed and Cort was told not to post rules. He took them down. "At the time I don't think I even argued with her," he mused, "so great was her authority among us. What it came down to was that the Catholic Worker was an extraordinary combination of anarchy and dictatorship."[25]

Dorothy disliked rules and regulations because she found them ineffective (HH, 125). She felt that personal example was the best way to influence people, agreeing with Peter Maurin that one ought to be what one wanted the other person to be. To this idea Cort responds:

> But in the real world of Mott Street you could throw good example at some people forever and watch it bounce off them like peanuts off a tank. And so a number of useful things did not get done, and some not-so-useful things did get done, because the people setting the good example were greatly outnumbered by the people setting bad example, or, more likely, just setting.[26]

Mark Ellis's experience corroborates Cort's. In addition to the obvious, creative tasks of writing, editing, placing paste-ups and printing, preparing the paper on a monthly basis required also the more tedious tasks of folding, addressing, applying stickers, sorting, tying in bundles, and mailing fifty thousand to a hundred thousand or more copies each month.[27]

---

25. John Cort, "My Life at the Catholic Worker," 364.
26. Cort, "My Life at the Catholic Worker," 364.
27. Nancy Roberts's excellent study provides information about the circulation of *The Catholic Worker* in an appendix to *Dorothy Day and the Catholic Worker*, 179–82.

Papers were brought in to the New York Catholic Worker house on a rented truck and had to be carried to the second floor to be prepared. Forming a line, Catholic Workers and street people would pass the bundles of papers (250 papers per bundle) from hand to hand. Ellis adds to this scene illuminating detail illustrating Catholic Worker belief in individual initiative and personal responsibility:

> The work is tiring. Volunteers, as well as people from the house, pitch in. Sometimes a Bowery person, after finishing his soup-meal, joins the line. . . . When people get tired and drop out of the line gaps develop and the load becomes heavier, especially when you have to walk upstairs to reach the next person. There is a wealth of labor on the first floor but no one is asked to help. Personal initiative only: not even a gentle coercion is allowed.[28]

Day herself would affirm these commentaries. In a 1961 entry in her column "On Pilgrimage," Day lamented the filth of the Chrystie Street house, offering vivid detail about the disadvantages of respecting human freedom (OPS, 67).

Dorothy's acceptance of people as they were had its limits, as John Cogley and other Chicago Catholic Workers found out when they voiced their sympathy for the allies entering the war against Hitler. It is claimed that the only thing like a split among Catholic Workers came as a result of the Catholic Worker's pacifist stand during World War II.[29] Day's position on war, stated forthrightly during the Spanish Civil War in September 1938, was clear and uncomplicated:

> "We are opposed to the use of force as a means of settling personal, national, or international disputes." As a newspaper trying to effect public opinion, we take this stand. We feel that if the press and the public throughout the world do not speak in terms of the counsels of perfection, who else will?[30]

Many of the most committed and energetic Workers were not pacifists as Dorothy was. Though some went to conscientious objector camps, many were drafted and others joined the army. Those who disagreed with Dorothy, those who became interventionists in the face of Hitler's threat, those who wrote their criticisms of the realism and rightness of

---

28. Marc Ellis, *A Year at the Catholic Worker*, 100.
29. Bruce Cook, "Dorothy Day and the Catholic Worker," 11.
30. Day, "Explains CW Stand on Use of Force," 4.

pacifism did so in places other than the New York *Catholic Worker*. John Cogley, perhaps the most vocal and visible of the dissidents on this matter, withdrew and with his withdrawal came the end of the Chicago Catholic Worker. Day grieved this loss and sought a context enabling her to accept it.

> It is a matter of grief to me that most of those who are Catholic Workers are not pacifists, but I can see too how good it is that we always have this attitude represented among us. We are not living in an ivory tower. [LL, 304]

Cogley found her attitude condescending and complained in a letter to Day that he resented her way of handling his dissent: namely, by accepting him and his position in a spirit of deliberate charity while at the same time refusing to deal with his objections to pacifism intellectually.[31]

She held fast to her pacifist stance. In 1945, she issued a condemnation of the U.S. use of the atom bomb with the use of irony:

> Mr. Truman was jubilant. President Truman. True man. What a strange name, come to think of it . . . Truman is a true man of his time in that he was jubilant. . . . We have killed 318,000 Japanese.
> That is, we hope we have killed them, the Associated Press . . . says. . . . It is to be hoped they are vaporized, our Japanese brothers, scattered, men, women and babies, to the four winds, over the seven seas. Perhaps we will breathe their dust into our nostrils, feel them in the fog of New York on our faces, feel them in the rain on the hills of Easton.[32]

In a 1946 issue of *Catholic C.O.*, Day pondered the motivations of those who accepted induction into World War II. She mused that they did so in part because of a "desire to share in the sufferings of others. They felt they could not bear to see the world convulsed in such pain without trying to share in its anguish." She saw "this desire to share in the miseries of others" to be a "very great and a very terrible temptation."[33]

This is a curious interpretation, given John Cogley's judgment that the conditions required by the justifiable war theory were present in the

---

31. Piehl, *Breaking Bread*, 157.
32. Day, "We Go on Record," 1.
33. Day, "Women and War," 6.

conflict with Hitler.[34] His decision to enlist and a like decision by others could reasonably be viewed as motivated by a desire to resist evil, to be part of a larger project that opposed Hitler and nazism. Yet Day interpreted this motivation to enlist as "a terrible temptation" to share in the misery of others. A clue to understanding this harsh judgment may be found in her own youthful experience, for this view has a precedent in *The Long Loneliness* where Day directed a similar criticism to herself: "Was [my] desire to be with the poor and the mean and the abandoned not mixed with a distorted desire to be with the dissipated . . . to be with the poor to indulge [my] own vices [?]" (LL, 68) Having brought a sense of self-critical reflection to her own sup-posedly noble desires, Day later directed a similar distrust to the supposedly courageous choices of others. Given her pacifist convic-tions, Dorothy was not easily persuaded that any effort to participate in killing could be redeemed by noble intent and she judged such noble intent to be vulnerable to self-deception and specious judgment.

More than two decades later she was still addressing the question as posed by a new generation of students. She exhorted them to exam-ine their motives and follow their consciences. If a man truly thinks he is combatting evil by engaging in war, "he must follow his conscience regardless of others." Yet one "always has the duty of forming his conscience by studying, listening, being ready to hear his opponents' point of view" (OPS, 254). Dorothy's work was to provide that alter-native. She was thereby challenged to live her conviction that dif-ferences of opinion stimulated clarification of thought and cultivated the art of human contacts (HH, 238).

These illustrations of Dorothy Day in debate with the state, in disagreement with her church's officers, and in dialogue with her house community can be viewed as of one piece if we focus our attention on the undergirding anarchist features of her thought. Although she pre-ferred the words *libertarian*, *decentralist*, and *personalist* to *anarchist*, Day's attraction to anarchism was an enduring one. With Peter Maurin and others, most notably Ammon Hennacy and Robert Ludlow, Doro-thy Day sought fundamental changes in the structure of society by minimizing the presence and power of the state and by arguing on behalf of personal initiative and responsibility expressed in direct ac-tion.[35]

Whether acting alongside of or in spite of Peter Maurin, Dorothy

---

34. Roberts, *Dorothy Day and the Catholic Worker*, 134.
35. Robert Ludlow and Ammon Hennacy's differences on the use of the term "anarchism" took shape in the pages of *The Catholic Worker*. See Ludlow's "A Re-evaluation," 3, 8, and Hennacy's "Christian Anarchism Defined," 3, 7.

Day believed in the power of the person as the starting point for the good society. Day described anarchism as being "personalist before it's communitarian": it "begins with living a disciplined life, trying to be what you want the other fellow to be."[36] Day admitted that although one must assume responsibility oneself, the fact is that many others will not. When they do not, one must simply try to understand them, given their sufferings and their backgrounds, and accept them.[37]

The decentralized, communitarian society these Catholic Workers desired was never envisioned in detail, never theoretically conceptualized. Their ideal society, in which it would be "easier for people to be good" was, rather, glimpsed, suggested, intimated on the basis of specific moral values and religiously grounded ideals which took expression in action, not theory. Anarchists are not so much politicians or sociologists as they are moralists; their stand is not so much political and economic as it is spiritual and ethical.[38]

For Day, action was the most powerful mediator of meaning. Not only was it at times unnecessary to speak; it was often enough inappropriate to speak, inappropriate to ask. The need to help pass the bundles of papers required no requests precisely because the need for help shouted itself to those within range. People then respond as they are able. Personal initiative only. No coercion allowed. Abilities and inclinations varied dramatically among people, given their capacities, histories, and opportunities. Day viewed personal example as the only trustworthy means of influencing others.

Described as "Head Anarch," "Abbess," and mother of a large, far-flung family, Dorothy Day had no interest in democratic processes where each cast a vote and the majority ruled. Wide-ranging discussion of meanings and elaboration of arguments were fine and encouraged in the round-table discussions. But she had her limits: certain convictions (pacifism, personalism, the centrality of the works of mercy) prevailed in the Worker publications as nonnegotiable and publicly expressed values. Certain behavioral assumptions pervaded life at the Catholic Worker, too, leading Day in the 1960s to dismiss some Workers whom she regarded as morally self-indulgent and undisciplined. Jim Forest's divorce and remarriage in 1967 moved Dorothy to request that Forest remove himself as head of the Catholic Peace Fellowship or she would remove her name from the list of sponsors.[39]

---

36. Doug Lavine, "Dorothy Day: 40 Years of Works of Mercy," 17.
37. Lavine, "Dorothy Day," 19.
38. Robert Ellsberg, "Sacco and Vanzetti," 2.
39. See Thomas Merton's correspondence with Dorothy Day, esp. 143–45, and with James Forest, 300–303, in William H. Shannon, ed., *The Hidden Ground of Love: The Letters of Thomas Merton.*

John Cort's description of the Catholic Worker as "an extraordinary combination of anarchy and dictatorship" is one Day would understand. A 1936 journal entry from Day:

> I am in the position of a dictator trying to legislate himself out of existence. They all complain that there is no boss. . . . Freedom—how men hate it and chafe under it, how unhappy they are with it![40]

Day's distrust of the political system is evident in her refusal to vote. This is in keeping with the antipolitical (not merely apolitical) feature of anarchism. To some, political authority is the root of all evil, tyrannous, no matter how democratic. Dorothy Day's view of political authority was less charged rhetorically; nonetheless she eschewed conventional political action because the government she observed was dominated by commercial and financial interests and deeply implicated in supporting the means of warfare. Furthermore, political, governmental, and other organizations made it all too easy to become immune to the needs of others and to be an excuse for personal inaction.[41] Day's commitment to a revolution from below led her to avoid politicians and heads of state and to look with a jaundiced eye on why anyone would want to work for the government.[42] Day's anarchist sensibilities also explain why the Catholic Worker as she led it was not a legal entity, offered no tax breaks for donors, held no policy meetings, and extended no votes.

Yet the question asked in the last chapter returns: How could Day have affirmed both anarchism and Catholicism simultaneously? Anarchism eschews rules and regulations except for the most minimal and necessary to make communes and cooperative arrangements work; Roman Catholicism is a highly complex organizational structure with myriad laws, obligations, and directives. Anarchism trusts and encourages individual freedom of choice, valued and understood within a radical awareness of human sociality, to be sure, but with a decided emphasis on freedom and individual judgment. Roman Catholicism, since the sixteenth century, has placed a decided emphasis on the symbolism and the authority of the pope and bishops who exercise authority in the name of Jesus the Christ. Day's religious sensibilities and the theology found in the social encyclicals led her to affirm and espouse a Christian anarchism which shared in common the principle

---

40. Dwight MacDonald, "The Foolish Things of the World," pt. 2, p. 52.
41. Mary Segers, "Equality and Christian Anarchism," 218.
42. Jim Wallis and Wes Michaelson, "Dorothy Day," 18.

of subsidiarity: "Popes and anarchists have emphasized the principle: subsidiarity. The State should never take over the functions that could be performed by a smaller body. The State should only enter when there are grave abuses."[43] Day's understanding of anarchism meant, above all, that everything began from the bottom up. What could be more "natural" to the Catholic church, she wondered, where "conscience is supreme"?[44] John Henry Newman's statement, "to conscience first, and to the Pope second" was one of Day's favorites.[45] "To us at the Catholic Worker, anarchism means 'Love God, and do as you will.' "[46]

Dorothy Day's reading of the centrality and supremacy of conscience as characteristic of the Catholic church is intriguing. Although the claim can indeed be defended in the history of Catholic theology, rooted in the thought of St. Paul and explicated in the theology of Thomas Aquinas, it is a claim that many nontheologically oriented practicing Catholics would find surprising. In pastoral practice, claims about the importance of conscience in the moral life of the individual are generally associated with the obligation to "inform" one's conscience with right thinking, the teaching of the church, and the natural law. One is then advised to "obey" the conscience which is also seen as a "law" which holds one to "obedience," for it is by that that one will be "judged."[47] Since she read the epistles of Paul and the writings of Thomas Aquinas after she met Peter Maurin, Day very likely delighted in their affirmations of conscience. But it seems equally likely that her esteem for conscience as central was originally rooted in her anarchist commitments and perhaps supplemented by her brief exposure to Episcopalianism.

Prince Peter Kropotkin, Russian revolutionist and anarchist, had been a central influence in Dorothy's life as a high school and college student. His call to live the law of conscience as opposed to the written laws of society appealed to Dorothy's heart and was accepted by her as a call to her youth. To live by the law of conscience was, for Kropotkin,

---

43. Studs Terkel interview with Dorothy Day in *Hard Times: An Oral History of the Great Depression*, 304.

44. Jeff Dietrich and Susan Polloch, "Dorothy Holds Forth," 1.

45. Dorothy Day, "Francis Cardinal McIntyre and the Duties of the Lay Catholic," 40.

46. Day, "On Pilgrimage," *The Catholic Worker*, July-August 1977, 2.

47. "The Pastoral Constitution on the Church in the Modern World," sec. 16, in Walter M. Abbott, S.J., ed., *The Documents of Vatican II* (New York: Guild Press, 1966), 213. See also vol. 4 of the *New Catholic Encyclopedia* (New York: McGraw-Hill, 1967) for articles on "Freedom of Conscience" by G. J. Dalcourt and "Conscience in the Bible" by E. R. Callahan.

to join the ranks of the revolutionists and work for the complete transformation of society (LL, 45–46). At one time Day felt his *Memoirs of a Revolutionist* was the most beautiful book she had ever read. The themes of struggle and decision which Kropotkin highlighted returned in Day's spiritual readings and spiritual counsel, under the direction of her spiritual advisor for many years, Father John J. Hugo, a priest of Pittsburgh, Pennsylvania.

Hugo emphasized the distinction and often the conflict between the natural and the supernatural dimensions of life to such an extent that some regarded his work as dangerously close to Jansenism. He was, together with his mentor, Father Onesimus Lacouture, reproached by church authorities and prevented from preaching his views at popular retreats. It is not my purpose to rehearse the details of this controversy,[48] but rather to note that this line of thinking, offering a sharp contrast between the natural and the supernatural, flesh and spirit, the world and the church, would have validated and intensified Day's previously articulated distrust of the state. Day's respect for Father Hugo continued in spite of his being silenced. Admitting that he and Father Lacouture might not have voiced their views in a manner that was theologically acceptable to the specialists, she remained grateful nonetheless for the spiritually liberating insights they gave her. Her social philosophy had been formed on themes of struggle, conflict, and opposition. These themes resonated powerfully as she sought to formulate a spiritual philosophy. The Catholic social teaching of the encyclicals, together with the Catholic theology and spirituality she appropriated, supported, enhanced, and justified her anarchism anew, giving it religious, spiritual, historical, and theological grounding.

Day and colleagues used the spirit and framework of anarchist thought to promulgate distributism as an alternative social philosophy to Marxist communism and American capitalism. Distributists wanted to distribute control as widely as possible by means of direct family ownership of land and capital. Ownership was essential for evoking responsibility. Although she consistently repudiated utopian thinking in her desire to be realistic and practical, Day was equally consistent in her conviction that God intended things to be much easier than people have made them. Though her preferred method of change was education, Day conceded that depression, war, hunger, and homelessness would eventually play their part in making it clear that there is some-

---

48. Brigid O'Shea Merriman's study of Day's spirituality, "Searching for Christ," provides the fullest discussion of this controversy. See also Miller, *Dorothy Day*, 335–41, and Fisher, *The Catholic Counterculture in America*, 54–60. See also John J. Hugo, *Applied Christianity*, for a statement of his theology.

thing inhuman about living in a city of ten million people. "Pope Pius XII pointed out that it was difficult for modern youth to live in the cities without heroic virtue." But "it was never intended that the good life should demand *heroic* virtue."[49]

Day was intrigued by the fact that although social commentators regularly critiqued distributism and sought to bury it, the discussion itself was evidence that distributism had not died. Nor would it die, she suggested, because distributism addressed the needs of man and his nature.[50] "Those who argue against it say it is impossible[,] not that it is undesirable. We say that it must be attempted."[51]

Anarchist historian George Woodcock claims that moral conviction is a pervasive though underexplored feature of anarchism, observing that the "anarchist believes in a moral urge powerful enough to survive the destruction of authority and still to hold society together in the free and natural bonds of fraternity."[52] Anarchist Day's exercise and understanding of power were suffused with moral motivation, moral value, and moral reflection. She believed preeminently in the power of persuasion by example—also by information, reflection, discussion, and examination—but by the example of direct action first and foremost. Such direct actions included the works of mercy by which the poor were fed, clothed, and sheltered. Direct action also included noncooperation with the state through the refusal to engage in military service, political service, jury service, payment of taxes. Theorists agree that the refusal to obey is the great weapon of the weak.[53] Combining this "weapon" with voluntary poverty freed Day and co-Workers to act from conscience rather than from wants, desires, and needs that constrict. Through noncooperation and voluntary poverty, Dorothy and friends rendered themselves both powerful and free.

The title of one of Day's pieces, "Without Poverty We Are Powerless," illustrates the great weight she placed on the power of voluntary poverty, the deliberate and intentional life choice of sharing whatever one had with those who had nothing. "While our brothers suffer from lack of necessities, we will refuse to enjoy comforts."[54] Day

---

49. Day, "Article on Distributism—2," 6. The discussion and debate on the philosophy of distributism recurred repeatedly throughout the history of the paper. The articles by Day listed in the Bibliography reflect this pattern. Day alludes to the long-term debate in "On Distributism—Answer to John Cort," 1, 3.

50. Day, "Distributism Is Not Dead," 4.

51. Day, "All the Way to Heaven is Heaven—Or, Article on Distributism—1," 7.

52. George Woodcock, *Anarchism*, 25.

53. Woodcock, *Anarchism*, 217; Gene Sharp, *The Politics of Nonviolent Action*; Elizabeth Janeway, *The Powers of the Weak*.

54. Day, "Poverty and Pacifism," 1.

felt that the works of mercy were the only bridge she had with the destitute, for the works of mercy enabled those with (food, clothing, shelter, money, talent, ability, desire) to share with those who were without. As highly as Day valued voluntary poverty, however, and as often as she spoke about it—often eloquently—she minced no words on the horror of the poverty of destitution as imposed by bureaucratic social structures and human indifference.[55] She never forgot the smell of poverty and in her writings sought to make it live before the eyes and noses of her readers. She wrote vividly, for example, about the terrible smell of dead rats in the walls of city dwellings—rats that could not be removed short of tearing down the house because no one could know for sure just where they were located (OP, 144–45). And she noted realistically that no matter how poor the facilities Catholic Workers lived in, no matter how meager the food, and how few the funds, Catholic Workers did not know destitution as did their many neighbors and guests, for the Workers enjoyed a sense of security that comes with community life (M, 52).

Power, poverty, and pacifism are thus intimately related in the moral vision of Dorothy Day. She urged her readers and fellow Workers to live the life of voluntary poverty as a way of resisting the war industry through the nonpayment of taxes and as a way of identifying and sharing with the poor: "Whatever you buy is taxed, so that you are, in effect, helping to support the state's preparations for war exactly to the extent of your attachment to worldly things of whatever kind."[56]

Living the life of the poor also clarified the purposes of labor. Jobs having to do with shelter, food, clothing, and the other works of mercy (instructing the ignorant, visiting the imprisoned, and the like) contributed to the common good and thus were rightly regarded as necessary and important. Jobs in advertising "which only increased people's useless desires" as well as in "insurance companies and banks, which are known to exploit the poor" did not contribute to the common good: "we pray God for the grace to give them up."[57]

Although Day hated utopian thinking and wanted above all to be practical, she was not inclined to apologize for her idealism. Consider-

---

55. Dorothy Day recognized human fault and limitation as partial causes for the misery she observed, but in her writings she focused on social structural problems and human indifference as the areas where change could occur. John Cogley's observation (*A Canterbury Tale*, 33) serves as a corrective to Day's emphasis:

> It was difficult for us to put all the blame on social disorders and none on man himself when we were hourly faced with the most unlovely exhibitions of human perversity—lying, cheating, duplicity, drunkenness, drug addiction.

56. In Robert Ellsberg, *By Little and By Little*, 111.
57. In Ellsberg, *By Little and By Little*, 1, 7.

ing it, rather, a "gift" and an "inspiration,"[58] she was convinced that life was not a matter of choosing between good and evil but of choosing between good and better.[59] Her sense that "God meant things to be much easier than we have made them" (OP, 102) functioned centrally in her vision and her daily work as writer, social activist, mother, pacifist, anarchist, resister. She measured her work by faithfulness rather than by statistics. Fidelity and constancy in love—by this measure, she believed, would people be judged. For all her disclaimers and self-criticisms, it is worth noting that she had no hesitation comparing herself to four of the most visible figures and arresting voices of modern Western history: "Of course we are few. But Marx and Engels and Trotsky and Stalin were few, but that did not keep them from holding *their* vision and studying and working toward it."[60] She knew she held a radical, revolutionary stance, a position consonant with, supported by, and integral to her identity and commitments as writer, mother, and religious inquirer.

---

58. Coles, *Radical Devotion*, 25.
59. In Ellsberg, *By Little and By Little*, 216.
60. In Ellsberg, *By Little and By Little*, 103.

5

THE MORALIST: MORAL AGENT AND MORAL ANALYST

I HAVE EXAMINED DOROTHY DAY'S WRITINGS with a twofold interest in how contemporary feminist questions serve to illuminate her thought and how, in turn, her work might contribute insight and self-critical reflection to current debates about and within feminist religious ethics. Taking her self-disclosure seriously, I have stayed in close range of her voice as starting point and reference point in order to note well her self-understandings and lines of thinking, modes of arguing, and forms of acting. In chapters one through four I have thereby sought to understand Dorothy Day through four lenses that she used to understand and present herself to readers: writer, woman, religious, and radical.

In this chapter, I add to these Day as moralist. As writer, as feminist ally and critic, as Roman Catholic believer, as radical anarchist, Day was drawn to and driven by moral concerns. She saw writing as an ethical response to what was going on in the world. She faulted and praised feminism on moral grounds, criticized religious leaders for moral tepidity and loved the encyclicals because of their moral and spiritual practicality. She esteemed anarchism precisely because it emphasized the moral power inherent in each person. Thus, although "moralist" was not a category she employed to describe herself, it is one we can trust she would affirm, for Dorothy Day regularly acknowledged the moral impulse that gave impetus to her work: to arouse the conscience.

In order to understand Day as moralist I wish to portray her moral vision and display her approach to moral questions with broad brush strokes, addressing additional issues of interest. For example, I am interested in how she regarded and approached the moral life, what she voiced as her program of action and what vision or world view underlay her actions. I want to note the religio-ethical norms that grounded her moral inquiry and reflection, the central sources she appealed to for ethical insight, and the distinctive context, tone, or style that marks her ethical thought and action. Also, I ask, what themes might we, students and scholars of Day, appropriate as we consider the relevance of her work for our time?

I understand ethics to be a process of inquiry and reflection through which a person attempts to bring sensitivity, disciplined thought, and discernment to the discovery of moral value. The process is religious ethics when the moralist, like Dorothy Day, thinks in terms of a religious world view, that is to say, thinks within, or out of, or in dialogue with a perspective that acknowledges an experience of ultimacy. The experience and perspective of ultimacy functions authoritatively in the sense that it compels attention: one seeks to make sense of it, respond appropriately in the face of it, utilize it as one among many resources available for information and insight in the process of coming to judgment and action. The experience of ultimacy together with attendant beliefs, feelings, and attitudes are not fixed, unquestioned givens but are themselves appropriate subjects of the critical reflection that constitutes ethics. Before her conversion, Day questioned religion as a Freudian and Marxist critic, deciding it was a prop the strong did not need and an opiate to the masses. After her conversion, she questioned the practice of religion against her ideals, regularly challenging and exhorting those who claimed to be religious. Although ethics in religious communities is commonly thought of as derivative of religious experience and expressive of religious beliefs and values, the reverse is also true. Religious convictions, beliefs, and practices are themselves apt subjects for ethical reflection and analysis. Dorothy was selective in the beliefs and practices she questioned, focusing on convictions with moral import such as pacifism, anarchism, and communitarianism. Theological convictions about the nature of God, sin, or grace were received as part of the gift of faith. Clear about the fact that she was not a theologian, she was not inclined to engage in theological debate.

Religious ethics is envisioned by some as concerned essentially with duties, obligations, and rights, addressing such questions as: What must I do? What rights are mine? What rights must I honor in others?

These questions reflect an imperative approach to ethical inquiry, imaging ethics in terms of commands and demands.[1] Religious ethics can also be seen as concerned essentially with values and virtues, focusing on unrealized possibilities rather than with "oughts." Within this framework the questions are: What can I do? How might I respond? What kind of society do we wish to create and become? How can I (we) best use my (our) powers? By focusing on ethical *possibilities* rather than ethical *obligations*, these questions alert us to a more open-ended, creative view of ethics. They express an indicative ethic of invitation rather than command, encouraging imaginative rather than conformist thought and behavior.

Both of these languages, the imperative and the indicative, are present in Dorothy Day's moral discourse. She employed the imperative when seeking to discern and determine how she herself ought to act: "the one thing we are sure of in feeding the unemployed is that our Lord wants us to do this work, so we must do it. We are liable to make mistakes in the paper, not being theologians or philosophers, nor experts in the line of economics and sociology; but we can make no mistake in feeding God's hungry ones" (HH, 242). With respect to others, however, she clearly favored the indicative mode, in keeping with her anarchist commitment to individual initiative and responsibility and her theological belief in the primacy of conscience. From this perspective, ethical response is limited only by a person's own ethical imagination, willingness, generosity, and courage. Day was clear that most of the choices we face in life are not between good and evil but between good and better (OP, 89). When she faulted herself for eating between meals, forgetting the starving millions around the world, she also faulted those who, hearing this, accused her of scruples rather than encouraging her to reach for her ideals (OP, 42–43). Day's writings thus appeal to possibilities and imperatives alike, are concerned with mights as well as with oughts, with coulds as well as with shoulds. "We must work from day to day in the tasks that present themselves," she wrote. "We have a program of action and a philosophy of life. The thing is to use them" (HH, 266).

Day's program of action was in part defined by Peter Maurin who proposed the publication and distribution of *labor papers*, the establishment of *houses of hospitality* for workers and the unemployed,

---

1. The description of ethics which follows is taken from my article "On Doing Religious Ethics." It has been reprinted with a new prefatory note, which makes explicit its connection with feminist ethics, in Andolsen et al., eds., *Women's Consciousness, Women's Conscience*, 265–84.

round-table discussions to encourage and enable the clarification of thought about questions pertaining to the social order, and the establishment of *farming communes*. Although Dorothy the journalist was most enthusiastic about the establishment of a labor paper and as reporter and editor was eager to encourage the clarification of thought, she accepted also his ideas about houses of hospitality and farming communes, personally adopting his four-point program. To these she added several points of her own: strikes, boycotts, reports on the daily lives of the destitute, exhortations to young men urging them to refuse conscription and to apply for conscientious objector status, civil disobedience, and its consequent imprisonment.

The *labor papers* that Maurin envisioned, unlike most papers, were not intended to report the news but rather to create news (M, 4) by providing a vision of a new social order informed by the social teaching of the Catholic church. Day, ever the reporter, combined these purposes by reporting on what *is* as well as what *ought* to be. To Peter's frustration and disappointment, she wrote about neighborhood news, legislative news, foreign policy news, and the like, though always within the advocacy context she and Peter shared. The *houses of hospitality* were intended to bring workers and scholars together to discuss Christian principles of cooperation and mutual aid as these were set forth in the papal encyclicals and to emphasize the importance of personal action and responsibility rather than reliance on political action and state responsibility (HH, 238). The *round-table discussions* were designed to provide settings where Peter could indoctrinate anyone willing to listen, where vigorous conversation with opposing positions could be voiced, where discussion and distribution of literature could take place, and where the "art of human contacts" could be cultivated (HH, 237–38, 158). Although dramatic differences often emerged in these settings, creating discomfort and disagreement, Dorothy valued them highly, feeling that "a great many truths came out in these arguments" (HH, 144). *Farming communes* were envisioned as places where the unemployed could be employed (there is never unemployment on the land, Peter had said) and where food would be grown for use at the houses of hospitality. These were the least successful element of the Catholic Worker program, and Dorothy herself admitted that as farmers, Catholic Workers were, in the main, ridiculous (LF, 50).

Permeating what must have been difficult, often discouraging work, was a vision, a cause, a project that gave Dorothy a "zest for life" (OP, 161). She was not satisfied merely to take care of "the wrecks of the social order" with palliatives. "What we need," she wrote, "is a revolution, beginning now" (OP, 98). It was the social order that she wished and worked to change (HH, 143). "It was, we conceded, the whole system that was out of joint. And it was to reconstruct the social order, that we were throwing ourselves in with the workers, whether in factories or shipyards or on the sea" (HH, 146). When the labor movement succeeded in organizing and making gains, Dorothy celebrated their successes, yet expressed ambivalence; to succeed was to run the risk of becoming part of the materialist and militarist system that always wanted more, a system and an attitude she continuously critiqued.

To display the ethic of Dorothy Day is to chart her program of action to be sure, but also to portray her underlying vision of life. For ethics is about seeing as well as about doing. Indeed it has rightly been said that "the basic vision of reality within which one thinks and experiences is more crucial for how ethical issues arise and are dealt with than is the formal analysis of moral experience."[2] How one sees life, envisions reality, names the good, the relationship between freedom and determinism, relationships among human beings and between human beings and the rest of nature, the place of and possibilities for truth, justice, care, and the like, will affect how one approaches, as well as resolves, ethical decisions. To look at Dorothy Day's ethical vision is to become conscious of the assumptions and presuppositions that comprised her world view and to notice what principles informed her moral imagination and guided her judgments. The Chinese proverb, that "two-thirds of what we see is behind our eyes," is an apt reminder to all of us to reflect similarly on the underlying assumptions of our own visions of life.

A number of convictions served as nonnegotiable principles for Day's interpreting and responding to social policy matters. Foremost among these was the dignity due the worker by virtue of being human and the honorable status of work, especially manual labor. Day viewed workers as partners with one another in a noble enterprise and she found it morally outrageous that workers should be viewed and treated as "chattel," as mere "muscle" and "physical power," or their work as a "commodity" by employers and others who needed and benefited from their labor (HH, 142, 143, 146). Day lamented that the major workers' representative, the American Federation of Labor, betrayed its constituents by failing to voice the fundamental principles of community and solidarity. Instead, it appealed to "enlightened self-interest,

---

2. John Cobb, Jr., "Response to Reynolds," in David Ray Griffin and Thomas J. J. Altizer, *John Cobb's Theology in Process* (Philadelphia PA: Westminster Press, 1977), 182.

a phrase reeking with selfishness" that functioned as a "warning and a threat" (HH, 146, 147) to workers that they were on their own as individuals with differing self-interests and not members of one another. She invoked the I.W.W. slogan, "an injury to one is an injury to all," and appealed to the metaphor of the Mystical Body, wherein all are seen as members of one another. When one member was affected, the whole body was affected (HH, 149).

Day's doctrine of "gentle personalism" (HH, 123) underscored the uniqueness of the individual and the dignity due the individual at the same time that it encouraged a communitarian view of life. Struggling to voice her position, Day found support in Karl Marx (from each according to ability and to each according to need) and the apostle Paul (let your abundance supply their wants) (HH, 123) as well as Peter Maurin and through him, Emmanuel Mounier. Mounier, a major voice of the personalist philosophy in France, defined the person as "a movement toward others," a "being-towards." His personalist philosophy affirmed the absolute value of the human person, describing the true personalist as one who assumes a stance of availability to others, examines her own life from the standpoint of others, relates to the other as subject rather than object, and takes upon herself the joys and troubles of the other in generosity and faithfulness.[3]

Placing high priority on the development of individual initiative and personal responsibility ("we try not to make rules, but look for individual initiative" [HH, 123]), Day believed that personal responsibility was itself stimulated by the ownership of necessities such as food, clothing, shelter, and land. Thus she approved of private property in moderation. Reflecting on the importance of the land, a key illustration of private property, Day used the rhetorical question to give praise to the earth: "What is more essential than the earth from which we all spring, and from which comes our food, our clothes, our furniture, our homes?" (OP, 107)

Day's pacifist commitments were based on common sense and the Sermon on the Mount.[4] She found it meaningless and unrealistic to pretend that any war (whatever it might be—against race, class, nation) could be the one war to end all wars, as the Marxists had maintained with respect to class war (HH, 148). War was the precise opposite of the works of mercy she valued so highly. Wars separated families, destroyed the land, rendered people hungry and homeless. How, she

---

3. Emmanuel Mounier, *Personalism*, 33, 21–22; John Hellman, *Emmanuel Mounier*.
4. Day, "Crusader in Exile," 22. See also Eileen Egan, "The Beatitudes, the Works of Mercy, and Pacifism."

wondered, could wars be seen to do any good? Robert Ellsberg describes Day's view of World War II: "In the long run, she believed, the effort to expunge the evil of Nazism by means of superior force would unleash on the world possibilities more terrible than anything known before."[5] Given the fears and criticisms generated by nuclear proliferation, many in our time would read her position as prophetic. Dorothy the revolutionary (HH, 239) named the revolution she fought for as a "revolution of love, instead of that of hate" (OP, 161). Her nonpassive pacifism used imagery of fighting without apology: indeed, "this fighting for a cause" (nonviolence) was "part of the zest of life" (OP, 98). But fighting and resisting by Day were always cast in nonviolent forms: written criticism, argumentation, and exhortation; participation in strikes; acts of civil disobedience; imprisonment and testimony; relocation in the face of cancellation; creation of alternative ways of living; works of mercy.

She hoped to voice a "theory of love" (OP, 161), a clarification of the reality of love, based on its practice. Day was seen by some as a sentimentalist, but she spoke sharply about love in markedly unsentimental language, giving a proper nod to *The Brothers Karamazov*: "love in action is a harsh and dreadful thing compared with love in dreams" (HH, 141). Also: "if you will to love someone, you soon do. You will to love this cranky old man and someday you do. It depends on how hard you try" (OP, 121). Love was what everyone wanted, she decided, "but it is hard to love in a two room apartment"—to which she added, "We are eminently practical, realistic" (OP, 102). Social change is thus required, for it was never intended that the good life should demand heroic virtue (OP, 107). Much of the misery she saw was caused by human decisions and social arrangements; these could be changed if there were sufficient desire and sheer, willed practice to change them. She wrote, marched, picketed, and civilly disobeyed in an effort to stimulate such desire. Driven by the fact that things could be otherwise, Day invited people to help her find ways to reconstruct the social order.

Day's world view was suffused with Christian and Catholic symbols (Father, Christ, Trinity, grace, prayer, works of mercy). She prayed to, thanked, and praised God for the faith tradition she prized. She believed that the "supernatural" gave "new powers" to that which was "natural" (OP, 114). For all her talk about human community, solidarity, and the will to love, she became convinced that without the Fatherhood of God there could be no brotherhood of man (HH, 187). This, then, became her linchpin: God as the grounding, origin, destiny, and model

---

5. Robert Ellsberg, *By Little and By Little*, xxxiii.

(revealed in Jesus) for human living. These convictions about the dignity of human life, the ennobling possibilities of human labor, the doctrine of gentle personalism, individual initiative to enhance community life, pacifism, the revolution of love, and the love of God modeled by Christ are the chief and abiding features of Day's world view or, in her words, her "philosophy of life." These convictions supported, nourished, and gave force to her program of action. Her ethic, like her editorial stance, was singularly consistent from 1933 to her death in 1980.[6] Those who knew her in community life use words other than consistency. Tom Cornell, an editor of *The Catholic Worker* in the early 1960s, alludes to her "intransigence" on the war issue regarding her differences with John Cogley and other workers who entered the armed services. She could be "fierce," "judgmental," and "hell on wheels," he told Nancy Roberts. Jim Forest, also an editor in the early 1960s, describes her as "uncommunicative" and "unimaginative in crisis," "stubborn" about fundamental convictions and similar to a "medieval bishop" in style.[7]

Day's decision processes, judgments, actions, and underlying moral vision thus display a complex yet distinctive ethic, which incorporates empathetic identification with the powerless and social criticism of the powerful who misused their power. Hers is an ethic that is built on moral desire for a society in which it is easier for people to be good and which uses the moral principles of care, justice, and communitarian personalism with revolutionary zeal, hope, and determination. For those of us who seek to identify, educate, and nurture talented students in educational settings, Day is a sobering reminder that the "unbright" and those broken in spirit not only require our attention, they can be our teachers. More to the point, in Day's view, they are our brothers and sisters, our mothers and fathers and children.

Ethicists commonly map ethical reasoning processes according to either a deontologist or consequentialist (e.g., utilitarian) typology—that is to say, according to the rightness of an action regardless of efficacious result expected or according to hope for a desired outcome or consequence, such as the increase or enhancement of happiness,

6. Nancy Roberts finds "the singular editorial consistency" of *The Catholic Worker* from 1933 to 1981 to be a rare phenomenon in American journalism history and the most important finding of her study (*Dorothy Day and the Catholic Worker*, 54). Colman McCarthy and Dwight MacDonald make similar observations about the consistency of her position ("Colman McCarthy on Dorothy Day," 32, and MacDonald, "Revisiting Dorothy Day," 12).

7. Tom Cornell, "The Catholic Church and Witness Against War," 201; also from an interview with Nancy Roberts in *Dorothy Day and the Catholic Worker*, 96; Jim Forest, "Dorothy Day," *Green Revolution*, 2,3.

justice, love, peace, or freedom. Dorothy Day's ethical orientation, attraction, and mode of thinking are deontological in the sense that she did have a sense of right action, feeling some imperatives from her given talents and chosen faith. She was not a consequentialist in the classic sense that she made her decisions or measured the appropriateness of her actions by a consequence quotient. She did not determine her actions or measure their effectiveness by visible results, but rather by constancy and fidelity to her ideals. Yet she did pay attention to results, particularly the results of human indifference and bureaucratic programs that failed the poor. Visible results were not the end of her decision/action process, but the beginning. Visible results moved her to act. Catholic Worker guests were a daily reminder to Day of the failure of government and of the need for personal initiative and direct action.

My view of ethics requires that in addition to judgment, action, and world view, we look also at the question of moral knowing. Having identified her convictions and program of action, it is appropriate to ask, how did Day know what she knew? On what grounds was she so sure, consistent, or stubborn? What were the sources of her convictions and why did she trust them? When Dorothy Day felt the limits of her knowledge from experience, conscience, and other people, she invoked faith, feeling that one *cannot expect* to understand everything. If one waited for understanding, one would never act (OP, 18, 39). Day the activist could not not-act. It would be incorrect to say that she valued action above knowledge, more accurate to say that she valued action *as a way of knowing*. She once told co-Worker and friend Stanley Vishnewski that she could only know what she had practiced (M, 3). Direct action, experience, practice—these constituted the source as well as the testing ground of insight and value.

This commitment to radical social action was itself propelled by intense and enduring feelings for others. "I always felt the common unity of our humanity" she wrote, then generalized, "the longing of the human heart is for this communion" (LL, 31). Day's life story is marked by intense feelings of unity, longing, joy, and mystery, but also by sadness, and even by terror.[8] Feelings mediated meaning for Dorothy Day, moving her toward religious conversion and from that to theological conviction; this in turn gave her a new language to voice an ethic long based on empathy for the disenfranchised. Mutual responsibility,

---

8. "Even as a little child of six I often awakened in the dark and felt the blackness and terror of nonbeing. I do not know whether I knew anything of death, but these were two terrors I experienced as a child, a terror of silence and loneliness and a sense of Presence, awful and mysterious" (OP, 47).

accountability, and community, characteristics of Day's native disposition and radical lifestyle, became deepened, supported, and renamed by the Catholic Christian social vision she appropriated. These ideals become cast as the love of God and neighbor, the centrality of the works of mercy, the theology of the Body of Christ, and the practice of prayer.

A fundamental weakness of the Catholic Worker movement, according to one critic, was its failure to articulate a theory of the good society it sought to create.[9] Given Day's activist bent, it is unlikely that she would concur that this judgment points to a weakness. But her stated critique, that she and her co-Workers sought to address too many needs and thus achieved too little by spreading their energies too far (LF, 192, 204), provides one important assessment of the movement's limitations and inadequacies. Her interest in creating the good society, or reconstructing the social order, however, also points to a potential point of contact with some feminist hopes for social reconstruction.

Although Dorothy Day did not ally herself publicly with any feminist communities or activities, and although she never articulated or appropriated a feminist perspective on society and history, her radical critique of social arrangements together with her desire to "reconstruct the social order" makes an alliance of her aspirations and many feminists' aspirations possible even now. Values that would enable conversation and cooperation between Dorothy Day and feminist Rosemary Ruether, for example, are evident in Ruether's response to the question: "What is the society we seek?"

> We seek a society that affirms the values of democratic participation, of the equal value of all persons as the basis for their civil equality and their equal access to the educational and work opportunities of the society. But more, we seek a democratic socialist society that dismantles sexist and class hierarchies, that restores ownership and management of work to the base communities of workers themselves, who then create networks of economic and political relationships. Still more, we seek a society built on organic community, in which the processes of childraising, of education, of work, of culture have been integrated to allow both men and women to share child nurturing and homemaking and also creative activity and decision making in the larger society. Still more, we seek an ecological society in which human and

---

9. William A. Au, *The Cross, the Flag, and the Bomb*, 31, 252.

nonhuman ecological systems have been integrated into harmonious and mutually supportive, rather than antagonistic, relations.[10]

Gerda Lerner's question, noted at the outset of this book, returns: What would history be like if seen through the eyes of Dorothy Day and ordered by the values she defined? It would, I propose, be very like the society described in Ruether's paragraph. Although Day would bring her editor's pen to Ruether's prose, deleting words like "democratic" and "socialist," in order to insert "anarchist" and "communitarian," there is a clear commonality of values and goals. What Ruether refers to as the "equal value of all persons" would, for Day, be the "respect and dignity" due all persons; what for Ruether are "sexist and class hierarchies" are for Day unfair expectations that limit women and men, unfair practices between labor and management, unwise and unbalanced emphases between worker and scholar. She would endorse Ruether's language about organic community and the integral connections among education, work, culture, and childrearing, about creative activity and decision making. She would very likely be present to help effect supportive rather than antagonistic relations among human and nonhuman systems.

Values shared with feminists Katie Cannon, Beverly Harrison, Carter Heyward, and Ada Maria Isasi-Diaz, for example,[11] provide further cause to imagine common agendas and collaboration with feminist-minded thinkers who, like Day, judge that some forms of feminism are rightly subject to criticism. Cannon and colleagues, for example, recognize the "morally ambiguous" history of feminism, faulting it for its racist and classist attitudes and calling it to root itself ever more deeply in the soil of abolition characteristic of its nineteenth-century expression. They acknowledge that some of the most vocal proponents of women's suffrage were indeed self-centered to the point of racism, that in an attempt to salvage women's rights in a sexist and racist society they turned their backs on black men and women.

Furthermore, some advocates of women's liberation in recent times have neglected to notice the race-, class-, culture-, and socioeconomic-specific features of their viewpoints, generalizing prematurely about "women's oppression" and "women's experience" without addressing significant historical, cultural, ethnic, and religious differences among

---

10. Ruether, *Sexism and God-Talk*, 232–33.
11. Also Bess B. Johnson, Mary D. Pellauer, and Nancy D. Richardson, all members of the Mudd Flower Collective and authors of *God's Fierce Whimsy*.

women. Many feminists thus encourage one another and, indeed, all
inquirers to use the nineteenth-century feminist-abolition alliance as a
resource for resisting racism in our time,[12] and to feed their thought
with information gathered from many cultures and conditions. As a
twentieth-century American woman with middle-class, Anglo-Saxon
roots, Dorothy Day is a striking model of one who refused to be defined
in inherited, socialized terms. Her empathy for the working class and
the underclass of diverse ethnic and racial backgrounds enabled her to
break through and out of the boundaries of that inherited identity. As
one who appreciated and chose to live with those who were without,
she demonstrated the possibility of turning nonpossession, nonattach-
ment, and lack of social prestige into strengths and virtues rather than
causes for embarrassment or denial. Her work urges us to notice that
people with possessions and status very often live in fear of losing these
and that such fear constricts vision and generosity.[13] Those without
goods, status, and prestige have little or nothing to lose and thus are
better poised to operate out of an ethic of sharing grounded in genuine
caring. Indeed, Day's views and values anticipate those voiced in the
liberation theologies of Latin America, Africa, and Asia: a decision to
see life from the standpoint of the poor and to stand with the poor in a
struggle for justice, an approach to theology rooted in praxis, a view of
religion as a spur to revolutionary action, a desire to help bring about
the transformation of society grounded in the values of justice, peace,
freedom, and love.

Looking at the goals of Dorothy Day and those of such feminists as
Ruether, Cannon, Harrison, Heyward, Isasi-Diaz, and others, presses
all of us to move beyond the polemical rhetoric and charged labels
(anarchist, socialist, feminist) and focus discussion and action on the
kind of persons we want to become and the kind of society we wish to
create. Dorothy Day's actions and writings call feminists of all persua-
sions, particularly those economically privileged, to demonstrate solidarity with women and men of all races, classes, and cultural
backgrounds in the United States and throughout the world by volun-
tarily relinquishing possessions or at least seeking to live simply—with
a diminished sense of acquisitiveness and an enhanced desire to
share—in order to live the future they wish to create.

Differences would not be erased. Dorothy Day's critical views of
extramarital sexual encounter, her discomfort with and disapproval of

12. See also Barbara Andolsen, "*Daughters of Jefferson*," and Bettina Apthecker,
Woman's Legacy.
13. For a more recent exploration of this theme, see Barbara Ehrenreich's *Fear of
Falling: The Inner Life of the Middle Class*.

lesbian lifestyle, and the social acceptance of abortion, for example, would likely remain unyielding points of difference with those feminists who support these options. Day's preferences for the poor and for action on behalf of the poor would very likely limit her tolerance for intellectual debate among the feminist intelligentsia. We can only wonder how she might respond to Sallie McFague's searching and searing theological analyses of common Christian images of God (as Father, King, and Judge) which Day accepted without question.[14] Similarly, we can only speculate how she might receive Mary Hunt's effort to relativize marriage and heterosexual relationships in general, and lift up for equal or greater value, other forms of friendship.[15]

Given her commitment to the disenfranchised *as* disenfranchised (regardless of gender) and her critique of the bourgeois, militarist, and materialist mentalities she despised, she would very likely insist on the need for human liberation (the liberation of women and men) without wishing to linger too long on women's liberation as such.

Feminists would look for evidence that Day could indeed grow to recognize the patriarchal features of Western philosophy and religion and the historically manifest sexism of her beloved Christian and Catholic traditions. Some would hope to expand her experience of religious conversion to conversion from the sexist thought patterns and expectations she inherited and sustained.[16] But the similarities of interest in personal and social transformation would surely move these women to talk to each other, recognize their solidarity on a number of fundamental hopes and goals, engage in round-table discussions about their differences, and in these ways achieve clarification of thought. They would then very likely be poised to decide together on strategies for direct action to arouse the conscience and improve the social order.

---

14. McFague, *Models of God.*
15. Hunt, *Fierce Tenderness.*
16. See, for example, Elisabeth Schüssler Fiorenza, "Sexism and Conversion."

BIBLIOGRAPHY

Andolsen, Barbara Hilkert. *"Daughters of Jefferson, Daughters of Boot-blacks": Racism and American Feminism*. Macon, GA: Mercer University Press, 1986.

———. "Gender and Sex Roles in Recent Religious Ethics Literature." *Religious Studies Review* 11, no. 3 (1985):217–23.

Andolsen, Barbara Hilkert, Christine E. Gudorf, and Mary D. Pellauer, eds. *Women's Consciousness, Women's Conscience: A Reader in Feminist Ethics*. New York: Seabury/Winston, 1985.

Apthecker, Bettina. *Woman's Legacy: Essays on Race, Sex, Class in American History*. Amherst, MA: University of Massachusetts Press, 1982.

Atkinson, Clarissa W., Constance H. Buchanan, and Margaret R. Miles, eds. *Immaculate and Powerful: The Female in Sacred Image and Social Reality*. Harvard Women's Studies in Religion Series. Boston: Beacon Press, 1985.

———, eds. *Shaping New Vision: Gender and Values in American Culture*. Harvard Women's Studies in Religion series. Ann Arbor, MI: UMI Research Press, 1987.

Au, William A. *The Cross, the Flag, and the Bomb: American Catholics Debate War and Peace, 1960–1983*. Westport, CT: Greenwood, 1983.

Avitabile, Alex. "*America* and the Early Years." *America* 127 (1972):396ff.

Banks, Olive. *Faces of Feminism: A Study of Feminism as a Social Movement*. Oxford: Martin Robertson, 1981.

Bass, Dorothy C., and Sandra H. Boyd. *Women in American Religious History: An Annotated Bibliography and Guide to Sources*. Boston: G. K. Hall, 1986.

Belenky, M. F., B. M. Clinchy, N.R. Goldberger, and J. M. Tarule, eds. *Women's Ways of Knowing: The Development of Self, Voice, and Mind*. New York: Basic Books, 1986.

Berrigan, Daniel, S.J. "A Day to Remember." *U.S. Catholic* 46 (1981):30–32.

Børreson, Kari. *Subordination and Equivalence in Nature: The Nature and Role of Women in Augustine and Thomas Aquinas*. Washington, DC: University Press of America, 1981.

Boulding, Elise. *The Underside of History: A View of Women Through Time*. Boulder, CO: Westview Press, 1976.

101

Brackley, Dean, and Dennis Dillon. "An Interview with Dorothy Day." *National Jesuit News*, May 1972, 8–10.

Buckley, William F. "The Catholic in the Modern World: A Conservative View." *Commonweal* 73 (1960):307–10.

Bynum, Caroline Walker. *Holy Feast and Holy Fast: The Religious Significance of Food to Medieval Women*. Berkeley: University of California Press, 1987.

————. "Women Mystics and Eucharistic Devotion in the Thirteenth Century." *Women's Studies* 11 (1984):179–214.

————. "Women's Stories, Women's Symbols: A Critique of Victor Turner's Theory of Liminality." In *Anthropology and the Study of Religion*, edited by Robert L. Moore and Frank E. Reynolds, 105–25. Chicago: Center for the Scientific Study of Religion, 1984.

Bynum, Caroline Walker, Steven Harrell, and Paula Richman, eds. *Gender and Religion: On the Complexity of Symbols*. Boston: Beacon Press, 1986.

Cahill, Lisa Sowle. *Between the Sexes: Toward a Christian Ethics of Sexuality*. Philadelphia, PA: Fortress Press, 1985.

Campbell, Debra. "The Catholic Earth Mother: Dorothy Day and Women's Power in the Church." *Cross Currents*, Fall 1984, 270–82.

Cambridge Women's Peace Collective. *My Country is the Whole World: An Anthology of Women's Work on Peace and War*. London: Pandora, 1984.

Carr, Anne. *Transforming Grace: Christian Tradition and Women's Experience*. San Francisco: Harper and Row, 1988.

Carroll, Berenice A. "Feminism and Pacifism: Historical and Theoretical Connections." In *Women and Peace: Theoretical, Historical and Practical Perspectives*, edited by Ruth Roach Pierson, 2–28. London: Croom Helm, 1987.

————, ed. *Liberating Women's History: Theoretical and Critical Essays*. Urbana, IL: University of Illinois Press, 1976.

Carroll, Berenice A., and Jane E. Mohraz, eds. " 'In a Great Company of Women': Nonviolent Direct Action." Special issue of *Women's Studies International Forum* 12, no. 1 (1988).

Carroll, Theodora F. *Women, Religion, and Development in the Third World*. New York: Praeger, 1983.

Chafe, William. *The American Woman (Her Changing Social, Economic, and Political Roles, 1920–1970)*. New York: Oxford University Press, 1972.

Chiu, Edmond. "Caring for Carers in a Fragmented World." *The Way: Contemporary Christian Spirituality* 28 (1988):342–47.

Chodorow, Nancy. *The Reproduction of Mothering*. Berkeley: University of California Press, 1978.

Christ, Carol. "The New Feminist Theology: A Review of the Literature." *Religious Studies Review* 3, no. 4 (1977):203–10.

Christ, Carol, and Judith Plaskow, eds. *Womanspirit Rising: A Feminist Reader in Religion*. San Francisco: Harper and Row, 1979.

Clark, Elizabeth, and Herbert Richardson, eds. *Women and Religion: A Feminist Sourcebook of Christian Thought*. New York: Harper and Row, 1977.

Cogley, John. *A Canterbury Tale: Experiences and Reflections 1916–1976*. New York: Seabury, 1976.

———. "A Harsh and Dreadful Love." *America* 127 (1972):394–96.

Coles, Robert. "Dorothy Day." *The New Republic* 184 (1981):28–32.

———. *Dorothy Day: A Radical Devotion*. Reading, MA: Addison-Wesley, 1987.

———. "In This Pagan Land." *America* 127 (1972):380-83.

———. *A Spectacle Unto the World: The Catholic Worker Movement*. New York: Viking, 1973.

Conn, Walter. "Bernard Lonergan's Analysis of Conversion." *Angelicum* 53 (1976):362–404.

———. *Christian Conversion: A Developmental Interpretation of Autonomy and Surrender*. New York: Paulist Press, 1986.

———, ed. *Conversion: Perspectives on Personal and Social Transformation*. Staten Island, NY: Alba House, 1978.

Cooey, Paula M., Sharon A. Farmer, and Mary Ellen Ross, eds. *Embodied Love: Sensuality and Relationship as Feminist Values*. San Francisco: Harper and Row, 1987.

Cook, Bruce. "Dorothy Day and the Catholic Worker." *U.S. Catholic* 31 (1966):6–14.

———. "The Real Dorothy Day." *U.S. Catholic* 31 (1966):25–31.

Cornell, Tom. "The Catholic Church and Witness Against War." In *War or Peace? The Search for New Answers*, edited by Thomas A. Shannon, 200–213. Maryknoll, NY: Orbis Books, 1980.

———. "Dorothy Day Remembered." *Sign*, June 1981, 5–10.

———. "Faith to Sustain a Vision and to Communicate It." *America* 127 (1972):390–91.

Cornell, Thomas C., and James H. Forest, eds. *A Penny a Copy: Readings from the Catholic Worker*. New York: Macmillan, 1968.

Cort, John C. "My Life at the Catholic Worker." *Commonweal* 107 (1980):361–67.

Cott, Nancy F. *The Grounding of Modern Feminism*. New Haven, CT: Yale University Press, 1987.

Curran, Charles E. *American Catholic Social Ethics: Twentieth Century Approaches*. Notre Dame, IN: University of Notre Dame Press, 1982.

———. "Christian Conversion in the Writings of Bernard Lonergan." In *Foundations of Theology: Papers from the International Lonergan Congress*, edited by Philip McShane, 41–59. Notre Dame, IN: University of Notre Dame Press, 1972.

Daly, Mary. *Beyond God the Father: Toward a Philosophy of Women's Liberation*. Boston: Beacon Press, 1973.

———. *Gyn/Ecology: The Metaethics of Radical Feminism*. Boston: Beacon Press, 1978.

Davis, Angela Y. *Women, Race and Class*. New York: Random House, 1981.

Day, Dorothy. " 'A.J.' [Muste]: Death of a Peacemaker." *Commonweal* 86 (1967):14–16.

———. "All in the Same Boat." *Newsday*, 16 March 1975, 1, 10–11.

———. "All the Way to Heaven is Heaven—Or, Articles on Distributism—1." *The Catholic Worker*, June 1948, 1,2,7.

————. "Anarchism through Peace." *The Catholic Worker* [Australia], August 1970, pp. 3–4.

————. "Article on Distributism—2." *The Catholic Worker*, July-August 1948, 1,2,6.

————. "The Case of Cardinal McIntyre." *The Catholic Worker*, July-August 1964, 1,6,8.

————. "A Catholic Looks at the Wars." *American Dialog* 2 (1965):3–5.

————. "A Catholic Speaks His Mind." *Commonweal* 55 (1952):640–41.

————. "Catholic Worker." *Res Ipsa Loquitur* 18 (1965):7–8.

————. "Conscience and Civil Defense." *New Republic* 133 (1955):6.

————. "Conversations on Distributism." *The Catholic Worker*, June 1955, 7.

————. "Crusader in Exile: A Visit With Robert Williams." *Liberation*, December 1962, 20–22.

————. "CW Refuses Tax Exemption." *The Catholic Worker*, May 1972, 1.

————. "Distributism is Not Dead." *The Catholic Worker*, July-August 1956, 4.

————. "Distributism vs. Capitalism." *The Catholic Worker*, October 1954, 1,6.

————. "Dorothy Day Writes From Jail." *The Catholic Worker*, July-August 1957, 3.

————. *The Eleventh Virgin*. New York: A. & C. Boni, 1924.

————. "Eviction." *Jubilee*, November 1958, 28–35.

————. "Explains CW Stand on Use of Force." *The Catholic Worker*, September 1938, 1,4,7.

————. "Fear in Our Time." In Proceedings of the Pax Conference October 1963, Spode House. Mimeographed. Dorothy Day-Catholic Worker Collection, Marquette University Library.

————. *Fight Conscription!* New York: The Catholic Worker, 1942.

————. "Francis Cardinal McIntyre and the Duties of the Lay Catholic." *Jubilee* 12 (1964):38–40.

————. *From Union Square to Rome*. New York: Arno Press, 1978 (reprint of the 1938 edition).

————. "Girls in Jail." *New Masses*, July 1928, 14,15.

————. "Have You Ever Been to Jail." *The Catholic Worker*, April 1950, 5.

————. "Having a Baby." *New Masses*, June 1928, 5–6. Reprinted in *The Catholic Worker*, December 1977, 8,7.

————. *House of Hospitality*. New York: Sheed and Ward, 1939.

————. "I Remember Peter Maurin." *Jubilee*, March 1954, 34–39.

————. "If Conscription Comes for Women." *The Catholic Worker*, January 1943, 1,4.

————. "The Incompatibility of Love and Violence." *The Catholic Worker*, May 1951, 1–2.

————. "Life of Prayer and Poverty." *The Catholic Worker*, February 1953, 2,6.

————. *Loaves and Fishes*. New York: Harper and Row, 1952.

————. *The Long Loneliness*. New York: Harper and Row, 1963.

————. "Love and Justice." *The Catholic Worker*, July-August 1952, 1–2.

————. *Meditations*, ed. Stanley Vishnewski. New York: Newman Press, 1970.

————. "Meditation on the Death of the Rosenbergs." Philadelphia, PA: American Friends Service Committee, 1953. Also in *The Catholic Worker*, July-August 1953, 2,6.

————. "More About Holy Poverty, Which Is Voluntary Poverty." *The Catholic Worker*, February 1945, 1.

————. "Mystery of the Poor." *The Catholic Worker*, April 1964, 2,8.

————. "No Party Line." *The Catholic Worker*, April 1952, 1,7.

————. "On Distributism: Answer to John Cort." *The Catholic Worker*, December 1948, 1,3.

————. *On Pilgrimage*. New York: Catholic Worker Books, 1948.

————. "On Pilgrimage." *The Catholic Worker*, April 1949, 1,2.

————. "On Pilgrimage." *The Catholic Worker*, January 1957, 1,2,8.

————. "On Pilgrimage." *The Catholic Worker*, 1970s, *passim*.

————. *On Pilgrimage: The Sixties*. New York: Curtis Books, 1972.

————. "People, Paper, and Work." *Grail*, April 1952, 1–7.

————. "Personalist Peter Maurin." *The Catholic Worker*, May 1953, 1–2.

————. "Peter and Women." *Commonweal*, December 1946, 118–91.

————. "The Pope and Peace." *The Catholic Worker*, February 1954, 1,7.

————. "Pope John XXIII: The Papacy and World Peace." *American Dialog*, July-August 1964, 8–10.

————. "Poverty and Destitution." *Dissent* 8(1961): 233–40.

————. "Poverty and Pacifism." *The Catholic Worker*, December 1944, 1,7.

————. "Poverty and Precarity." *The Catholic Worker*, May 1952, 2,6.

————. "Poverty Incorporated." *The Catholic Worker*, May 1950, 1–2.

————. "Poverty Is the Face of Christ." *The Catholic Worker*, December 1952, 3,6.

————. "Poverty Is the Pearl of Great Price." *The Catholic Worker*, July-August 1953, 1,7.

————. "Poverty Is to Care and Not to Care." *The Catholic Worker*, April 1953, 1,5.

————. "Poverty Without Tears." *The Catholic Worker*, April 1950, 1,3,5.

————. "Problems of the Pacifist." *Life of the Spirit* 8 (1953):245–52.

————. "Radical but not Communist." *The Catholic Worker*, July-August 1933, 5.

————. "Reflections on the Connection." *The Catholic Worker*, July-August 1960, 2,7.

————. "Remembering St. Francis." *St. Anthony Messenger*, October 1965, 38.

————. "A Reminiscence at 75." *Commonweal* 98 (1973):424–25.

————. "The Satan Bomb." *The Catholic Worker*, March 1950, 2.

————. "Some Random Thoughts on Poverty." *Marriage* 46 (1964):20–25.

————. "Southern Pilgrimage." *Commonweal* 74 (1961): 10–12.

————. "The Spirit of Violence." *The Catholic Worker*, September 1954, 1,8.

————. *Thérèse*. Notre Dame, IN: Fides, 1960.

————. "This Money Is Not Ours." *The Catholic Worker*, September 1960, 1.

———. "Thoughts After Prison." *Liberation*, September 1957, 5–7, and October 1957, 17–19.

———. "Vocation to Prison." *The Catholic Worker*, September 1957, 1,2,6.

———. "Voluntary Poverty." *The Catholic Worker*, July-August 1939, 4–5.

———. "We Go On Record." (Hiroshima and Nagasaki) *The Catholic Worker*, September 1945, 1.

———. "We Know What Poverty Is." *Witness* 3 (1966):3,8.

———. "What Do the Simple Folk Do?" *Church Society for College Work Report* 31 (1973):3–6.

———. "Where Are the Poor?" *The Catholic Worker*, January 1955, 1,6.

———. "Where Are the Poor? They Are in Prison Too." *The Catholic Worker*, July-August 1955, 1,8.

———. "Without Poverty We Are Powerless." *The Catholic Worker*, May 1948, 2,7.

———. "Women and War." *Catholic C.O.*, Fall 1946, 4,6.

———. "Wonderful Adventures." *Fellowship* 41 (1975):7,9.

———. "The Work of Dorothy Day in the Slums." *Catholic World* 170 (1950):333–37.

Degen, Marie Louise. *The History of the Woman's Peace Party*. New introduction by Blance Wiesen Cook. New York: Garland, 1972.

Devaney, Sheila Greeve. "The Limits of the Appeal to Women's Experience." In *Shaping New Vision: Gender and Values in American Culture*, edited by Clarissa W. Atkinson, Constance H. Buchanan, and Margaret R. Miles, 31–49. Ann Arbor, MI: UMI Research Press.

Dietrich, Jeff, and Susan Pollack. "Dorothy Holds Forth." *Catholic Agitator* 1 (1971):1–2.

Douglas, James. "Dorothy Day and the City of God." *Social Justice Review* 54 (1961):40–43.

Driver, Ann Barstow. "Review Essay: Religion." *Signs: Journal of Women in Culture and Society* 2, no. 2 (1976):434–42.

Dulles, Avery, S.J. "Fundamental Theology and the Dynamics of Conversion," *The Thomist* 45, no. 2 (April 1981):175–93.

Eck, Diana L., and Devaki Jain, eds. *Speaking of Faith: Global Perspectives on Women, Religion, and Social Change*. Philadelphia, PA: New Society Publishers, 1987.

Egan, Eileen. "The Beatitudes, the Works of Mercy, and Pacifism." In *War or Peace? The Search for New Answers*, edited by Thomas A. Shannon, 169–87. Maryknoll, NY: Orbis Books, 1980.

———. *Dorothy Day and the Permanent Revolution*. Erie, PA: Pax Christi, U.S.A., 1983.

———. "The Final Word Is Love." *Cross Currents* 30 (1980–81):377–84.

Ehrenreich, Barbara. *Fear of Falling: The Inner Life of the Middle Class*. New York: Pantheon, 1989.

Eisenstein, Hester, and Alice Jardine, eds. *The Future of Difference*. New Brunswick, NJ: Rutgers University Press, 1987.

Eisenstein, Zillah. *Feminism and Sexual Equality: Crisis in Liberal America.* New York: Monthly Review Press, 1984.

————, ed. *Capitalist Patriarchy and the Case for Socialist Feminism.* New York: Monthly Review Press, 1979.

Ellis, Marc. *Peter Maurin: Prophet in the Twentieth Century.* New York: Paulist Press, 1981.

————. *A Year at the Catholic Worker.* New York: Paulist Press, 1978.

Ellsberg, Robert. "Sacco and Vanzetti." *The Catholic Worker*, July-August 1977, 1–2.

————, ed. *By Little and By Little: The Selected Writings of Dorothy Day.* New York: Alfred A. Knopf, 1983.

Elshtain, Jean Bethke. *Public Man, Private Woman: Women in Social and Political Thought.* Princeton, NJ: Princeton University Press, 1981.

Elshtain, Jean Bethke, and Sheila Tobias, eds. *Women, Militarism, and War: Essays in History, Politics, and Social Theory.* Totowa, NJ: Rowman and Littlefield, 1990.

Ethen, Jeff. "Portrait of a Christian Radical." *St. Cloud Visitor*, 3 November 1983, 11.

Farley, Margaret. "New Patterns of Relationship: Beginnings of a Moral Revolution." In *Woman: New Dimensions*, edited by Walter Burghardt, S.J., 51–70. New York: Paulist Press, 1977.

————. *Personal Commitments: Making, Keeping, Breaking.* Minneapolis, MN: Seabury, 1986.

————. "Sources of Sexual Inequality in the History of Christian Thought." *Journal of Religion* 56 (1976):162–76.

Finn, James. "Religion and a Catholic Worker [Dorothy Day]." *Worldview*, February 1981, 18.

Fiorenza, Elisabeth Schüssler. *In Memory of Her: A Christian Theological Reconstruction of Christian Origins.* New York: Crossroad, 1983.

————. "Sexism and Conversion," *Network Quarterly* 9, no. 3 (May-June 1981):15–22.

Fisher, James Terence. *The Catholic Counterculture in America, 1933–1962.* Chapel Hill, NC: University of North Carolina Press, 1989.

Fitch, Bob. "Dorothy Day: Witness to a Radical Faith." *Youth*, May 1973, 34ff.

Flynn, Elizabeth Gurley. *The Alderson Story: My Life as a Political Prisoner.* New York: International Publishers, 1963.

————. *The Rebel Girl: An Autobiograhy: My First Life 1906–1926.* New York: International Publishers, 1973.

————. *Words on Fire: The Life and Writings of Elizabeth Gurley Flynn*, edited by Rosalyn Fraad Baxandall. New Brunswick, NJ: Rutgers University Press, 1987.

Forest, Jim. "Dorothy Day." *Green Revolution* 21 (1973):2–3.

————. *Love Is the Measure: A Biography of Dorothy Day.* New York: Paulist Press, 1986.

————. "The Roots of Catholic Resistance." *Catholic World* 214 (1971):61–65.

Frary, Tom. " 'Thy Kingdom Come'—The Theology of Dorothy Day." *America* 127 (1972):385–88.

Fremantle, Anne. "She is the Most Unsentimental of Saints." *America* 127 (1972):388–89.

French, Marilyn. *Beyond Power: On Women, Men, and Morals.* New York: Summit Books, 1985.

Friedman, Jean E., and William G. Shade. *Our American Sisters: Women in American Life and Thought.* Boston: Allyn and Bacon, 1973.

Furfey, Paul Hanly. *Fire on the Earth.* New York: Arno Press, 1978.

———. "From a Catholic Liberal into a Catholic Radical." *America* 127 (1972):392–93.

———. Letter to His Eminence William Cardinal O'Connell, Archbishop of Boston, October 30, 1935. Dorothy Day-Catholic Worker Collection, Marquette University Library.

———. *Love and the Urban Ghetto.* Maryknoll, NY: Orbis Books, 1978.

Garvey, Michael. *Confessions of a Catholic Worker.* Chicago, IL: Thomas More Press, 1978.

Giles, Mary E., ed. *The Feminist Mystic and Other Essays on Women and Spirituality.* New York: Crossroad, 1982.

Gilligan, Carol. *In a Different Voice.* Cambridge, MA: Harvard University Press, 1982.

———. "Moral Orientation and Moral Development." In *Women and Moral Theory,* edited by Eva Feder Kittay and Diana T. Meyers, 19–33. Totowa, NJ: Rowman and Littlefield, 1987.

Gilligan, Carol, Janie Victoria Ward, and Jill McLean Taylor, eds. *Mapping the Moral Domain: A Contribution of Women's Thinking to Psychological Theory and Education.* Cambridge, MA: Center for the Study of Gender, Education and Human Development, 1988.

Goldman, Emma. *Anarchism and Other Essays.* 3rd revised edition. New York: Mother Earth, 1917.

Gregory, Judith. "Remembering Dorothy Day." *America* 144 (1981):344–47.

Griffin, Emilie. *Turning: Reflections on the Experience of Conversion.* Garden City, NY: Doubleday, 1980.

Grimshaw, Jean. *Feminist Philosophers: Women's Perspectives on Philosophical Traditions.* Sussex, UK: Wheatsheaf, 1986. Published in the United States as *Philosophy and Feminist Thinking.* Minneapolis, MN: University of Minnesota Press, 1986.

Gross, Rita, ed. *Beyond Androcentrism: New Essays on Women and Religion.* Missoula, MT: Scholars Press, 1977.

Gross, Rita M., and Nancy A. Falk, eds. *Unspoken Worlds: Women's Religious Lives in Non-Western Cultures.* San Francisco: Harper and Row, 1980.

Gunn, Janet Varner. *Autobiography: Toward a Poetics of Experience.* Philadelphia, PA: University of Pennsylvania Press, 1982.

Haddad, Yvonne Y., and Ellison B. Findly, eds. *Women, Religion, and Social Change.* Albany, NY: State University of New York Press, 1985.

Haddon, Genia Pauli. *Body Metaphors: Releasing God-Feminine in Us All.* New York: Crossroad, 1988.

Harding, Sandra. "The Curious Coincidence of Feminine and African Moralities." In *Women and Moral Theory*, edited by Eva Feder Kittay and Diana T. Meyers, 296–315. Totowa, NJ: Rowman and Littlefield, 1987.

Harding, Sandra, and Merrill B. Hentikka, eds. *Discovering Reality: Feminist Perspectives on Epistemology, Metaphysics, Methodology, and Philosophy of Science.* London: D. Reidel, 1983.

Harrison, Beverly. *Making the Connections: Essays in Feminist Social Ethics*, edited by Carol S. Robb. Boston: Beacon Press, 1985.

Haughton, Rosemary. *The Transformation of Man: A Study of Conversion and Community.* Springfield, IL: Templegate, 1967.

Held, Virginia. "Feminism and Moral Theory." In *Women and Moral Theory*, edited by Eva Feder Kittay and Diana T. Meyers, 111–28. Totowa, NJ: Rowman and Littlefield, 1987.

Hellman, John. *Emmanuel Mounier and the New Catholic Left, 1930–1950.* Toronto: University of Toronto Press, 1981.

Hennacy, Ammon. *The Book of Ammon: Autobiography of a Catholic Anarchist.* New York: Catholic Worker Books, 1965. Published earlier under the title *Autobiography of a Catholic Anarchist.* Glen Gardener, NJ: Libertarian Press, 1954.

———. "Christian Anarchism Defined." *The Catholic Worker*, July-August 1955, 3,7.

Heyward, Carter. *Our Passion for Justice: Images of Power, Sexuality, and Liberation.* New York: Pilgrim Press, 1984.

———. *The Redemption of God: A Theology of Mutual Relation.* Washington, DC: University Press of America, 1982.

Hill, Thomas E., Jr. "The Importance of Autonomy." In *Women and Moral Theory*, edited by Eva Feder Kittay and Diana T. Meyers, 129–38. Totowa, NJ: Rowman and Littlefield, 1987.

Hooks, Bell. *Ain't I a Woman: Black Women and Feminism.* Boston: South End Press, 1981.

———. *Feminist Theory: From Margin to Center.* Boston: South End Press, 1984.

———. *Talking Back: Thinking Feminist, Thinking Black.* Boston: South End Press, 1989.

Hugo, John J. *Applied Christianity.* New York: D.J. Fiorentino, 1944.

———. "The Immorality of Conscription." *The Catholic Worker*, April 1948, 3–10.

Hunt, Mary E. *Fierce Tenderness: A Feminist Theology of Friendship.* New York: Crossroad/Continuum, 1990.

Jain, Devaki. "Gandhian Contributions Toward a Feminist Ethic." In *Speaking of Faith: Global Perspectives on Women, Religion and Social Change*, edited by Diana L. Eck and Devaki Jain, 275–91. Philadelphia, PA: New Society Publishers, 1987.

Janeway, Elizabeth. *Man's World, Woman's Place: A Study in Social My-thology.* New York: William Morrow, 1971.

———. *Powers of the Weak.* New York: Alfred A. Knopf, 1980.

Jelinek, Estelle C. *The Tradition of Women's Autobiography: From Antiquity to the Present.* Boston: Twayne, 1986.

———, ed. *Women's Autobiography: Essays in Criticism.* Bloomington, IN: Indiana University Press, 1980.

Jessup, Hubert D. "Dorothy Day and Simone Weil: The Fruits of Religious Conviction." In *Simone Weil: Live Like Her?*, edited, transcribed, and introduced by George Abbot White. Cambridge, MA: M.I.T. Press, 1976. Manuscript in the Dorothy Day-Catholic Worker Collection, Marquette University Library.

Iones, Mother (Mary Harris Jones). *Autobiography of Mother Jones.* Chicago: Charles H. Kerr & Company, 1925.

———. *Mother Jones Speaks: Collected Writings and Speeches,* edited by Philip S. Foner. New York: Monad Press, 1983.

Kagawa, Toyohiko. *Brotherhood Economics.* New York: Harper and Row, 1936.

Kent, Edmond, S.J. "Dorothy Day: An Interview." *Studies: An Irish Quarterly Review* 39 (1950):174–86.

Kimerman, Leonard I., and Lewis Perry, eds. *Patterns of Anarchy.* Garden City, NY: Anchor, 1968.

Kittay, Eva Feder, and Diana T. Meyers, eds. *Women and Moral Theory.* Totowa, NJ: Rowman and Littlefield, 1987.

Klejment, Anne, and Alice Klejment. *Dorothy Day and the Catholic Worker: A Bibliography and Index.* New York: Garland, 1986.

Kolbenschlag, Madonna. *Kiss Sleeping Beauty Good-Bye: Breaking the Spell of Feminine Myths and Models.* Garden City, NY: Doubleday, 1979.

Kohlberg, Lawrence. "Moral Stages and Moralization: The Cognitive-Developmental Approach." In *Moral Development and Behavior: Theory, Research, and Social Issues,* edited by Thomas Lickona, 31–53. New York: Holt, Rinehart and Winston, 1976.

———. *The Philosophy of Moral Development: Moral Stages and the Idea of Justice.* San Francisco: Harper and Row, 1981.

———. *The Psychology of Moral Development: The Nature and Validity of Moral Stages.* San Francisco: Harper and Row, 1984.

Kollias, Karen. "Class Realities: Create a New Power Base." *Quest,* Winter 1975, 28–43.

Kraditor, Aileen S. *The Ideas of the Woman Suffrage Movement 1890–1920.* New York: Columbia University Press, 1965.

———. "Woman Suffrage in Perspective." In *Our American Sisters: Women in American Life and Thought,* edited by Jean E. Freidman and William G. Shade, 219–30. Boston: Allyn and Bacon, 1973.

Lamb, Matthew L. *Solidarity with Victims: Toward a Theology of Social Transformation.* New York: Crossroad, 1982.

Lane, Belden C. "Precarity and Permanence: Dorothy Day and the Catholic Worker Sense of Place." In *Landscapes of the Sacred: Geography and Narrative in American Spirituality*, 161–83. New York: Paulist Press, 1988.

Langland, Elizabeth, and Walter Gove, eds. *A Feminist Perspective in the Academy: The Difference It Makes.* Chicago: University of Chicago Press, 1983.

Lavine, Doug. "Dorothy Day: 40 Years of Works of Mercy." *National Catholic Reporter*, 8 June 1973, 1.

LeBrun, John Leo. "The Role of the Catholic Worker Movement in American Pacifism, 1933–1972." Ph.D. diss., Case Western University, 1973.

Lerner, Gerda. *The Creation of Patriarchy.* New York: Oxford University Press, 1986.

————. *The Female Experience: An American Documentary.* Indianapolis, IN: Bobbs-Merrill, 1977.

————. *The Majority Finds Its Past: Placing Women in History.* New York: Oxford University Press, 1979.

————. *The Woman in American History.* Menlo Park, CA: Addiston-Wesley, 1971.

Linner, Rachelle. "Bread and Roses [Voluntary Poverty]." *Katallagete* 8 (1982):19–28.

Lobue, Wayne. "Public Theology and the Catholic Worker." *Cross Currents* 26 (1976):270–85.

Lonergan, Bernard. *Method in Theology.* London: Darton,Longman, and Todd, 1971.

————. "Natural Right and Historical Mindedness." *Proceedings of the American Catholic Philosophical Association* 51 (1977):132–43.

————. "Theology in Its New Context." In *A Second Collection*, edited by W. F. J. Regan and B. J. Tyrrell, 55–67. London: Darton, Longman, and Todd, 1974.

Ludlow, Robert. "A Re-evaluation." *The Catholic Worker*, June 1955, 3,8.

MacDonald, Dwight. "The Foolish Things of the World." *New Yorker*, pt. 1, 4 October 1952, 37–56; pt. 2, 11 October 1952, 37–52.

————. "Revisiting Dorothy Day." *New York Review of Books*, 28 January 1971, 14–19. Same as "Introduction" to the clothbound facsimile edition-reprint of *The Catholic Worker*, 1–12. Westport, CT: Greenwood, 1970.

Maguire, Daniel C. *The Moral Revolution: A Christian Humanist Vision.* San Francisco: Harper and Row, 1986. See especially chap. 9, "The Feminization of God and Ethics," 105–21; chap. 10, "The Feminist Turn in Ethics," 122–29; chap. 11, "The Exclusion of Women from Orders: A Moral Evaluation," 130–40.

Marciniak, Ed. "Constancy to the Church and Social Teaching." *America* 127 (1972):393.

Marsh, Margaret. *Anarchist Women 1870–1920.* Philadelphia, PA: Temple University Press, 1981.

Mason, Mary G. "The Other Voice." In *Autobiography: Essays Theoretical and Critical*, edited by James Olney, 207–35. Princeton, NJ: Princeton University Press, 1980.

Massey, Marilyn. *Feminine Soul: The Fate of an Ideal.* Boston: Beacon Press, 1985.

Maurin, Peter. *Easy Essays.* Chicago: Franciscan Herald Press, 1984.

Mayer, Milton. "A Dollar for Dorothy." *The Progressive* 41 (1977):40–41.

———. "God's Panhandler." *The Progressive* (1981): 14–15.

McAllister, Pam. *Reweaving the Web of Life: Feminism and Nonviolence.* Philadelphia, PA: New Society Publishers, 1982.

McCarthy, Abigail. "Confronting Dorothy Day." *Commonweal* 104 (1977):297,317–18.

McCarthy, Colman. "Colman McCarthy on Dorothy Day," *New Republic*, 24 February 1973, 30–33.

McFague, Sallie. "Conversion: Life on the Edge of a Raft." *Interpretation* 32 (1978):255–68.

———. *Models of God: Theology for an Ecological, Nuclear Age.* Philadelphia, PA: Fortress Press, 1987.

McGowan, Patricia. "Somebody Loves You When You're Down and Out." *U.S. Catholic* 40 (1975):28–31.

McMillan, Carol. *Women, Reason and Nature: Some Philosophical Problems with Feminism.* Princeton, NJ: Princeton University Press, 1982.

McNeal, Patricia F. *The American Catholic Peace Movement 1928–1972.* New York: Arno Press, 1978.

Merriman, Brigid O'Shea. "Searching for Christ: The Spirituality of Dorothy Day (1897–1980)." Ph.D. diss., Graduate Theological Union, Berkeley, 1989.

Michaelson, Wes. "Encountering Dorothy Day: Angry but Obedient Daughter of the Church." *Sojourners* 5 (1976):17–18.

Miles, Margaret. *Fullness of Life: Historical Foundations for a New Asceticism.* Philadelphia, PA: Westminster Press, 1981.

Miller, William. *A Harsh and Dreadful Love: Dorothy Day and the Catholic Worker Movement.* New York: Liveright, 1973.

———. *All Is Grace: The Spirituality of Dorothy Day.* Garden City, NY: Doubleday, 1987.

———. "The Church and Dorothy Day." *Critic* 35 (1976):62–70.

———. "Dorothy Day and the Bible." In *The Bible and Social Reform*, edited by Ernest R. Sandeen, 155–78. Chico, CA: Scholars Press, 1982.

———. *Dorothy Day: A Biography.* San Francisco: Harper and Row, 1982.

———. "Dorothy Day, 1897–1980: All Was Grace." *America* 143 (1980):382–86.

Mollenkott, Virginia Ramey, ed. *Women of Faith in Dialogue.* New York: Crossroad, 1987.

Moore, Arthur J. "Dorothy Day and the Catholic Worker: Understanding an Icon." *Christianity and Crisis* 43 (1983):260–62.

Moraga, Cherrie, and Gloria Anzaldua, eds. *This Bridge Called My Back: Writings by Radical Women of Color.* Waterdown, MA: Persephone Press, 1981.

Morris, John. *Versions of the Self*. New York: Basic Books, 1966.

Mounier, Emmanuel. *Personalism*. New York: Grove Press, 1950.

Mud Flower Collective, The. *God's Fierce Whimsy: Christian Feminism and Theological Education*. New York: Pilgrim Press, 1985.

Murray, Pauli. "Black Theology and Feminist Theology: A Comparative View." *Anglican Theological Review* 60, no. 1 (January 1978):3–24.

Nails, Debra, Mary Ann O'Loughlin, and James Walker, eds. Special issue on "Women and Morality." *Social Research* 50 (1983).

National Conference of U.S. Catholic Bishops. *The Challenge of Peace: God's Promise and Our Response*. Boston: St. Paul Editions, 1983.

Neal, Marie Augusta. "Social Encyclicals: The Role of Women." *Network Quarterly* 3, no. 2 (Spring 1975):1–8.

Nicholson, Linda J. "Women, Morality, and History," *Social Research* 50, no. 3 (Autumn 1983):514–36.

Noddings, Nel. *Caring: A Feminine Approach to Ethics and Moral Education*. Los Angeles: University of California Press, 1984.

Novitsky, Anthony. "Peter Maurin's Green Revolution: The Radical Implications of Reactionary Social Catholicism." *Review of Politics* 37 (1975):83–103.

O'Brien, David J. "The Pilgrimage of Dorothy Day." *Commonweal* 107 (1980):711–15.

———. *The Renewal of American Catholicism*. New York: Oxford University Press, 1972.

Ochs, Carol. *Women and Spirituality*. Totowa, NJ: Rowman and Allanheld, 1983.

O'Connor, June. "Dorothy Day and Gender Identity: The Rhetoric and the Reality." *Horizons: Journal of the College Theology Society* 15, no. 1 (Spring 1988):7–20.

———. "Dorothy Day as Autobiographer." *Religion*, 18 (July 1990):275–95.

———. "Dorothy Day's Christian Conversion." *The Journal of Religious Ethics* 18, no. 1 (Spring 1990):159–80.

———. "Liberation Theologies and the Women's Movement: Points of Comparison and Contrast." *Horizons, The Journal of the College Theology Society* 2, no. 1 (Spring, 1975):103–15.

———. "On Doing Religious Ethics." *The Journal of Religious Ethics* 7, no. 1 (Spring 1979):81–96. Reprinted in *Women's Consciousness: Women's Conscience*, edited by Barbara Hilkert Andolsen, Christine Gudorf, and Mary Pellauer, 265–84. New York: Seabury/Winston, 1985.

———. "Process and Liberation Theologies: Theological and Ethical Reflections." *Horizons, The Journal of the College Theology Society* 7, no. 2 (Fall 1980):231–47.

———. *The Quest for Political and Spiritual Liberation: A Study in the Thought of Sri Aurobindo Ghose*. Madison, NJ: Fairleigh Dickinson University Press; London: Associated University Presses, 1977.

———. "Rereading, Reconceiving, and Reconstructing Traditions: Feminist

Research in Religion." *Women's Studies: An Interdisciplinary Journal* 17, nos. 1 and 2 (1989):101–23.

———. "Sensuality, Spirituality, Sacramentality." *Union Seminary Quarterly Review* 40, nos. 1 and 2 (1985):59–70.

O'Gorman, Ned. "A Bit Like a Serpent, a Bit Like a Dove." *America* 127 (1972):392–93.

Olney, James. "Autobiography and the Cultural Moment: A Thematic, Historical, and Bibliographical Introduction." In *Autobiography: Essays Theoretical and Critical*, edited by James Olney, 3–27. Princeton, NJ: Princeton University Press, 1980.

Patrick, Anne E. "Women and Religion: A Survey of Significant Literature, 1965–1974." *Theological Studies* 36, no. 4 (1975):737–65.

Pellauer, Mary. "Moral Callousness and Moral Sensitivity: Violence Against Women." In *Women's Consciousness, Women's Conscience*, edited by Barbara Hilkert Andolsen, Christine Gudorf, and Mary Pellauer, 33–50. New York: Seabury, 1985.

Piehl, Mel. *Breaking Bread: The Catholic Worker and the Origin of Catholic Radicalism in America*. Philadelphia, PA: Temple University Press, 1982.

Pius XII, Pope. "Christmas Message, December 23, 1956, The Contradiction of Our Age." *The Pope Speaks* 3, no. 4 (1957):331–46.

Plaskow, Judith. "The Feminist Transformation of Theology." In *Beyond Androcentrism: New Essays on Women and Religion*, edited by Rita Gross, 23–33. Missoula, MT: Scholars Press, 1977.

Purpura, Mary. "Dorothy Day: Legacy of a Catholic Radical." B.A. thesis, Wesleyan University, Middletown, CT, 1984. Dorothy Day-Catholic Worker Collection, Marquette University Library.

Quigley, Margaret, and Michael Garvey, eds. *The Dorothy Day Book*. Springfield IL: Templegate, 1982.

"Radical Nonviolence." *Christopher Closeup*. Interview of Dorothy Day and Thomas Cornell, 20 October 1971. Videotape in the Dorothy Day-Catholic Worker Collection, Marquette University Library.

Raymond, Janice G. *A Passion for Friends: Toward a Philosophy of Female Affection*. Boston: Beacon Press, 1986.

Reinhold, H.A. "The Long Loneliness of Dorothy Day." *Commonweal* 55 (1952):521–22.

Ricoeur, Paul. *Hermeneutics and the Human Sciences: Essays on Language, Action, and Interpretation*. Edited, translated, and introduced by John B. Thompson. Cambridge: Cambridge University Press, 1981.

Roberts, Nancy L. "Building a New Earth: Dorothy Day and the "Catholic Worker." *Christian Century* 97 (1980):1217–21.

———. *Dorothy Day and the Catholic Worker*. Albany, NY: State University of New York, 1984.

Rogers, Herbert W. "The Obedient but Angry Daughter of Holy Church." *America* 127 (1972):389–90.

Rosenberg, R. *Beyond Separate Spheres: Intellectual Roots of Modern Feminism*. New Haven, CT: Yale University Press, 1982.

Rowland, Robyn, ed. *Women Who Do and Women Who Don't: Join the Feminist Movement.* London: Routledge and Kegan Paul, 1984.

Ruddick, Sara. *Maternal Thinking: Toward a Politics of Peace.* Boston: Beacon Press, 1989.

Ruether, Rosemary Radford. "Christianity." In *Women in World Religions,* edited by Arvind Sharma, 207–33. Albany, NY: State University of New York Press, 1987.

————. "The Feminist Critique in Religious Studies." In *A Feminist Perspective in the Academy: The Difference It Makes,* edited by Elizabeth Langland and Walter Gove, 52–66. Chicago: University of Chicago Press, 1981.

————. "The Future of Feminist Theology in the Academy." *Journal of the American Academy of Religion* 53 (December 1985):703–13.

————. "Home and Work: Women's Roles and the Transformation of Values." In *Woman: New Dimensions,* edited by Walter J. Burghardt, S.J., 71–83. New York: Paulist Press, 1977.

————. "The Question of Feminism." In Rosemary Radford Ruether, *Disputed Questions: On Being a Christian,* 109–42. Nashville, TN: Abington Press, 1982.

————. *Sexism and God-Talk: Towards a Feminist Theology.* Boston: Beacon Press, 1983.

————. "Spirit and Matter, Public and Private: The Challenge of Feminism to Traditional Dualisms." In *Embodied Love: Sensuality and Relationship as Feminist Values,* edited by Paula M. Cooey, Sharon A. Farmer, and Mary Ellen Ross, 65–76. San Francisco: Harper and Row, 1987.

————. "Women and Peace." In *Women's Consciousness, Women's Conscience,* edited by Barbara Hilkert Andolsen, Christine Gudorf, and Mary Pellauer, 63–74. New York: Seabury/Winston, 1985.

————, ed. *Religion and Sexism: Images of Woman in the Jewish and Christian Traditions.* New York: Simon and Schuster, 1974.

Ruether, Rosemary Radford, and Rosemary Skinner Keller, eds. *Women and Religion in America,* 3 vols. San Francisco: Harper and Row, 1981, 1983, 1986.

Ruether, Rosemary Radford, and Eleanor McLaughlin, eds. *Women of Spirit: Female Leadership in the Jewish and Christian Traditions.* New York: Simon and Schuster, 1979.

Russell, Letty M. *The Future of Partnership.* Philadelphia, PA: Westminster Press, 1979.

————. *Household of Freedom: Authority in Feminist Theology.* Philadelphia, PA: Westminster Press, 1987.

Russell, Letty M., Kwok Pui-lan, Ada Maria Isasi-Diaz, and Katie Geneva Cannon, eds. *Inheriting Our Mothers' Gardens: Feminist Theology in Third World Perspective.* Philadelphia, PA: Westminster Press, 1988.

Saiving, Valerie. "Androcentrism in Religious Studies." *The Journal of Religion* 56 (1976):177–97.

————. "The Human Situation: A Feminine View." *The Journal of Religion* 40 (1960):100–12.

Sandberg, John Stuart. "The Eschatological Ethic of the Catholic Worker." S.T.D. diss. Catholic University of America, 1979.

Sayre, Robert. "Religious Autobiography." In *Encyclopedia of the American Religious Experience: Studies of Traditions and Movements*, 3 vols., edited by Charles H. Lippy and Peter W. Williams, 2:1223–36. New York: Charles Scribner's Sons, 1988.

Scherer, Peggy. "Living the Gospel." In *Once a Catholic*, edited by Peter Occhiogrosso, 102–18. Boston: Houghton Mifflin, 1987.

Schlissel, Lillian, ed. *Conscience and America: A Documentary History of Conscientious Objection in America 1757–1967*. New York: E. P. Dutton and Co., 1968.

Segers, Mary C. "Equality and Christian Anarchism: The Political and Social Ideas of the Catholic Worker Movement." *Review of Politics* 40 (1978):196–230.

Segundo, Juan Luis. *The Liberation of Theology*. Maryknoll, NY: Orbis Books, 1976.

Shannon, William H., ed. *The Hidden Ground of Love: The Letters of Thomas Merton on Religious Experience and Social Concerns*. New York: Farrar, Straus, Giroux, 1985.

Sharma, Arvind. *Women in World Religions*. Albany, NY: State University of New York Press, 1987.

Sharp, Gene. *The Politics of Nonviolent Action*. Boston: Porter Sargent, 1973.

Shatz, Marshall S. "Introduction." In *The Essential Works of Anarchism*, edited by Marshall S. Shatz, xi–xxix. New York: Quadrangle Books, 1972.

Sher, George. "Other Voices, Other Rooms? Women's Psychology and Moral Theory." In *Women and Moral Theory*, edited by Eva Feder Kittay and Diana T. Meyers, 178–89. Totowa, NJ: Rowman and Littlefield, 1987.

Sherry, George. "The More Common It Becomes, the More Holy It Becomes: An Interview with Dorothy Day." *Georgia Bulletin*, 11 February 1965, 3.

Shuster, George N. "Only One Candle in an Immense and Impenetrable Darkness." *America* 127 (1972):388.

Sklar, Kathryn Kish. "The Last Fifteen Years: Historians' Changing Views of American Women in Religion and Society." In *Women in New Worlds: Historical Perspectives on the Wesleyan Tradition*, 2 vols., edited by Hilah F. Thomas and Rosemary S. Keller, 1:48–65. Nashville, TN: Abingdon Press, 1981.

Smith, Sidonie. *A Poetics of Women's Autobiography*. Bloomington, IN: Indiana University Press, 1987.

Soelle, Dorothee. *The Strength of the Weak: Toward a Christian Feminist Identity*, translated by Robert and Rita Kimber. Philadelphia, PA: Westminster Press, 1984.

Spacks, Patricia Meyer. "The Difference It Makes." In *A Feminist Perspective in the Academy: The Difference It Makes*, edited by Elizabeth Langland and Walter Gove, 7–24. Chicago: University of Chicago Press, 1981.

Spender, Dale. *Man Made Language*. Boston: Routledge and Kegan Paul, 1980.

————. *Women of Ideas: And What Men Have Done to Them from Aphra Behn to Adrienne Rich.* London: Routledge and Kegan Paul, 1982.

————, ed. *Feminist Theorists: Three Centuries of Key Women Thinkers.* New York: Pantheon Books, 1983.

————, ed. *Men's Studies Modified: The Impact of Feminism on the Academic Disciplines.* New York: Pergamon Press, 1981.

Spengemann, William C. *The Forms of Autobiography: Episodes in the History of a Literary Genre.* New Haven, CT: Yale University Press, 1980.

Spretnak, Charlene, ed. *The Politics of Women's Spirituality: Essays on the Rise of Spiritual Power within the Feminist Movement.* Garden City, NY: Anchor/Doubleday, 1982.

Starrett, Barbara. "The Metaphors of Power." In *The Politics of Women's Spirituality: Essays on the Rise of Spiritual Power within the Feminist Movement*, edited by Charlene Spretnak, 185–93. Garden City, NY: Anchor/Doubleday, 1982.

"Still a Rebel." *Bill Moyers' Journal* (Public Broadcasting Service), 20 February 1973. Videotape in the Dorothy Day-Catholic Worker Collection, Marquette University Library.

Stocker, Michael. "Duty and Friendship: Toward a Synthesis of Gilligan's Contrastive Moral Concepts." In *Women and Moral Theory*, edited by Eva Feder Kittay and Diana T. Meyers, 56–68. Totowa, NJ: Rowman and Littlefield, 1987.

Storkey, Elaine. *What's Right With Feminism.* Grand Rapids, MI: William B. Eerdman Publishing Co., 1985.

Sturzo, Luigi. *Inner Laws of Society: A New Sociology.* New York: P. J. Kennedy and Sons, 1944.

Terkel, Studs. *Hard Times: An Oral History of the Great Depression.* New York: Pantheon, 1970.

Trask, Haunani-Kay. *Eros and Power: The Promise of Feminist Theory.* Philadelphia, PA: University of Pennsylvania Press, 1986.

Trible, Phyllis. *God and the Rhetoric of Sexuality.* Philadelphia, PA: Fortress Press, 1978.

Vishnewski, Stanley. "Dorothy Day: A Sign of Contradiction." *Catholic World*, August 1969, 203–6.

————. "Life in Community." *The Catholic World*, 185 (1957):346–51.

————. "Radicals of the Right." *Grail* 35 (1953):48–52.

————. *Wings of the Dawn.* New York: The Catholic Worker, 1984.

Wallis, Jim, and Wes Michaelson. "Dorothy Day: Exalting Those of Low Degree." *Sojourners* 5 (1976):16–19.

Ware, Ann Patrick. "Change and Confrontation within the Roman Catholic Church." In *Women of Faith in Dialogue*, edited by Virginia Ramey Mollencott, 29–41. New York: Crossroad, 1987.

Ware, Susan. *Holding Their Own: American Women in the 1930s.* Boston: Twayne, 1982.

Weaver, Mary Jo. *New Catholic Women: A Contemporary Challenge to Traditional Religious Authority.* San Francisco: Harper and Row, 1985.

Welch, Sharon. *Communities of Resistance and Solidarity: A Feminist Theology of Liberation*. Maryknoll, NY: Orbis Books, 1985.

Williams, Michael A., ed. *Charisma and Sacred Biography*. Vol. 48 of the Journal of the American Academy of Religion Thematic Series. Decatur, GA: Scholars Press, 1982.

Willock, Ed. "Dorothy Day and the Family." *Torch*, June–July 1954, 7–9.

Wills, Garry. *Bare Ruined Choirs: Doubt, Prophecy, and Radical Religion*. New York: Delta, 1972.

————. "Dorothy Day at the Barricades." *Esquire* 100 (1983):228–32.

Woodcock, George. *Anarchism: A History of Libertarian Ideas and Movements*. New York: Penguin, 1979.

Yates, Gayle Graham. "Spirituality and the American Feminist Experience." *Signs: Journal of Women in Culture and Society* 9, no. 1 (1983):59–72.

Zahn, Gordon. *Another Part of War: The Camp Simon Story*. Amherst, MA: University of Massachusetts Press, 1979.

————. "Leaven of Love and Justice." *America* 127 (1972):383–85.

Zaretsky, Eli. *Capitalism, the Family, and Personal Life*. Rev. and exp. ed. New York: Harper and Row, 1986.

Zinsser, William. *Inventing the Truth: The Art and Craft of Memoir*. Boston: Houghton Mifflin, 1987.

INDEX

119

theology of, 52
in *Union Square*, 19–20, 51
Cornell, Tom, 94
Cort, John, 76, 81

Day, Dorothy
  Catholic Church and, 57–59, 71–75
  early adulthood of, 18–19
  The Eleventh Virgin, 13–18, 22–23, 29, 36, 44
  empathy of, 59–60, 63, 65, 98
  ethics of, 50–51, 87–99
  faithfulness and, 30, 86
  feelings of, 64–65, 95
  feminism and, 38, 42–43, 45, 96, 97–99
  friendships of, 25–26
  From Union Square to Rome, 14, 22–23, 51
  "gentle personalism" and, 92
  "Having a Baby," 55
  imprisonment of, 34–35, 39–40, 68–69
  inner unity of, 31
  Loaves and Fishes, 14, 26–29, 40
  The Long Loneliness, 14, 22–23, 44, 79
  on love, 93
  as mother, 49, 54–55
  Mothers for Peace and, 74–75
  pacifism of, 69–70, 77, 78, 93
  Pius XII and, 71–72
  radicalism and, 24, 30, 67–86
  relationships with
    Batterham, 19, 22, 24, 37, 54–56
    her father, 39
    Maurin, 13, 24–25, 27, 40–41, 79, 89–90
    men, 24–25
    women, 25–26
  self-perception of, 11, 12, 30, 32, 49, 50
  sexuality and, 44, 98–99
  state power and, 68–71
  voluntary poverty and, 71, 84–85
  "Without Poverty We Are Powerless," 84
  on women, 47–48
  work and, 31–33, 45–47, 91
  writing and, 29–30
Debs, Eugene, 21
Della (Day's sister), 57
Deontology, 94–95
Disarmament, 72
Distributism, 43, 83, 84
Dostoyevsky, Feodor Mikhailovich, 21
  The Brothers Karamazov, 93

Eleventh Virgin, The (Day), 13–18, 22–23, 29, 36, 44
Ellis, Marc, 46, 76
Ellsberg, Robert, 61
Emotions, 64–65
Empathy, 59–60, 63, 65, 98
Encyclicals, 41, 74
Enlightenment, The, 5–6
Episcopalianism, 82
Ethics, 50–66, 87–99
  feminist, 6–7
    Day's moral vision and, 51
    social injustices and, 41
    women's experience and, 48
  religious, 88–89
Example, persuasion by, 77, 80, 84
Extramarital sexuality, 98

Faithfulness, 30, 86
Farming communes, 90
Fatherhood of God, 93–94
Feeding the hungry, 41
Feelings, 64–65, 95
Feminism
  Day and, 38, 42–43, 45, 96, 97–99
  Marsh on, 36
  Pellauer on, 4–5
  religion and, 6–7
  social injustices and, 41
  social revolutions and, 5–6
Feminist ethics, 6–7